HAUNTED SURREY

HAUNTED
SURREY

Rupert Matthews

The
History
Press

First published 2011

The History Press
The Mill, Brimscombe Port
Stroud, Gloucestershire, GL5 2QG
www.thehistorypress.co.uk

British Library Cataloguing in Publication Data.
A catalogue record for this book is available from the British Library.

ISBN 978 0 7524 5634 8
Typesetting and origination by The History Press

Contents

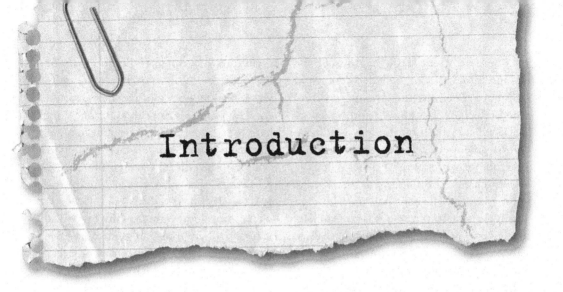

Introduction

I was born in Surrey and have lived most of my life here — as I still do.

I grew up learning the ghost stories of the village where I lived. When I was at school every child knew that there was a house behind a shop in the High Street that was haunted, though nobody seemed to know by what. We all avoided it. And in another house, we were told, a woman had once seen a vision of a friend at the instant that friend died. Two miles away was a pub said to be haunted by a serving girl from years past. A girl I was at school with had a grandfather who had worked at the pub and knew all about the ghost. She walked the upstairs rooms, swishing her long silk skirts against the walls and slamming doors shut. Spooky stuff.

As I grew older my interest in ghosts and the supernatural did not wane and over the years I have collected hundreds of stories about the ghosts of Surrey. I have talked to dozens of people who have had first-hand encounters with the phantoms of the county. This book is the result. Some of the tales date back some years, others are very recent. Generally I have avoided repeating tales about private houses, though a few outstanding examples are included, and have concentrated on the phantoms that frequent the sorts of public places and buildings where you would be welcome to visit.

Surrey is a varied county, each area having its own character. The county originated as the 'southern region' of the Kingdom of the Middle Saxons in about 550 at which time it extended into parts of what are now Hampshire and Berkshire, and reached along the Thames right up to the south side of London Bridge. By about 860 it had shrunk to the boundaries that it enjoyed until the spreading suburbs caused the north-eastern corner of the county to be shifted into London in the nineteenth century.

There are three basic sections of the county, though I have included a fourth in this book. These are the lowlands north of the high chalk hills known as the Downs, the lowlands south of the Downs and the Downs themselves. The lowlands north of the hills form part of the Thames Valley, the River Thames forming the northern edge of the county. The soils here are light and easily farmed, so the area was traditionally the most prosperous area of the county. To the east the soils became sandier and unpopulated heath land predominates. The hills themselves are dominated by chalk grassland that was traditionally grazing land for sheep, but more recently has been used for horseracing, cricket and housing. The lowlands south of the Downs is underlain by clay, giving a dense and boggy soil that has only recently been much use for farming. Traditionally it was covered by the ancient forest known as the Weald.

Cutting through the Downs is the River Wey, opening up a route through the hills that has been used by generations of travellers. The modern rail and road links still use it. The county town of Guildford grew up by the gap in the hills, and until the growth of the London suburbs was the largest town in Surrey. In this book, Guildford has a section to itself. This is not because it is important, bustling and prosperous — though it is — but because it is seething with ghosts, phantoms and spooks of all kinds.

The ghosts and phantoms of Surrey are no less varied than the landscape that they inhabit. There are spectres of the rich and famous to be encountered – Sir Thomas More, Field Marshal Ligonier and Bonnie Prince Charlie among them – but there are also the wraiths of penniless peddlers and struggling workmen to be met. Some of Surrey's ghosts are inoffensive and retiring. Others are undeniably scary – and even terrifying. Most seem to be going about the county on business of their own without taking any notice of we mere mortals who glimpse them from time to time. And there is no shortage of these supernatural inhabitants. More than once, I pulled up in a village to investigate some ghost or other only to find that other spectres and phantoms had their haunts there.

The companion volume to this book that I have also written for The History Press is entitled *Paranormal Surrey*. That book had a section on ghosts which gave details on some ghosts of Surrey. I have not given those stories again in great detail here and would urge you to get hold of a copy of that book as it gives not only greater detail on some hauntings, but also has chapters on UFOs, cryptozoology, fairies and other bizarre happenings in the county.

I must thank the people of Surrey both for their help in putting this book together and for their unfailing courtesy toward a traveller in search of spooks and ghosts. Some have been happy for me to quote them talking about their experiences, and I thank them for that. Others have preferred to remain anonymous, which is fair enough and I have respected their choice.

I will close with a simple observation. It is all very well reading about ghosts and spectres, but there is nothing to compare with actually getting out to visit the haunted site itself. Even when the ghost does not put in an appearance itself, there is some intangible and yet very real atmosphere to these places that can be fully appreciated only during a visit. I would urge all readers to get out on the road to investigate these haunted places for themselves.

With a county as beautiful and welcoming as Surrey it would be an effort amply rewarded.

Rupert Matthews, 2011

1

The Thames Valley

WE start our tour of haunted Surrey in the far north-eastern corner, on the fringe of the county that is being swallowed up by London. It was in 1889 that areas of Surrey such as Vauxhall, Brixton and Lambeth were transferred to the newly created London County Council. In 1965 Sutton, Croydon, Kingston and neighbouring areas left Surrey to become part of the Greater London Council, much larger than its predecessor. That left Surrey with pretty much the boundaries that it has now.

Thames Ditton

Barely a hundred yards from the new London-Surrey border is to be found the first of the Surrey ghosts. This is a gentle lady dressed in a flowing white gown who walks about the rooms and corridors of the Home of Compassion in Thames Ditton. A friend of mine worked there as a volunteer nurse for a few years back in the 1980s and vouched for the reality of the phantom. Other evidence comes in the form of a striking photo taken in 1925 by local historian T.S. Mercer. Mercer had been selected to record a series of murals painted by a Sister Miriam in the chapel. At the time, Mercer noticed nothing unusual, but when the pictures were developed one of them showed a semi-transparent whitish figure. Mercer had his camera and the negative carefully studied by experts to rule out any mishap, and they concluded that the camera had caught something that was really there.

The white lady is generally said to be the ghost of Pamela Fitzgerald. Mrs Fitzgerald had led an adventurous life - being the daughter of a French aristocrat executed during the Revolution. She was married to an actor shot dead in an Irish rebellion and she travelled widely through Europe. She retired to Thames Ditton in the 1820s as the property was then owned by relatives of her dead husband. Her grave is in the nearby churchyard.

The Marquis of Granby Public House

South of Thames Ditton stands the ancient coaching Inn of the Marquis of Granby overlooking the busy Scilly Isles roundabout where five roads meet and rush hour traffic is always congested. The pub was

The Marquis of Granby, an old coaching inn between Esher and Thames Ditton. The rather confused story of the ghost here may be related to an outbreak of poltergeist activity.

built in the seventeenth century and its ghost dates to not long after. The most often reported spectre here is that of a servant girl who died in the inn in vague but macabre circumstances some time in the eighteenth century. If she is a servant, she is an odd one, for she wears a heavy silk gown that can be heard rustling as she walks.

One account has the poor girl meeting her death after being locked in an upstairs cupboard by the landlord. He had, apparently, fallen in love with the pretty girl and objected to her wasting her time and affections on a penniless lad who worked in the stables. There is no real evidence for the tale, so it may be a confusion with the other ghost at the Marquis of Granby.

Sometime in the nineteenth century the pub was attacked by what was then called a demon. Reading the fragmentary accounts that survive, the entity sounds more like a poltergeist — one of those troublesome visitors that smash glasses, hide keys, throw objects about, make loud noises and generally disrupt life for months on end before departing as mysteriously as they arrive. A local clergyman was called in and apparently exorcised the demon into a cupboard on the first floor. He jammed the cupboard door shut with a Bible and sternly forbade anyone to open the door. As far as I know, nobody has dared touch it since.

Esher

South-west along the old Portsmouth Road, now bypassed by the dual-carriageway A3, lies the village of Esher, where I grew up. My old school still overlooks the village green, though it is now an Adult Education Centre, but other old properties have gone. Among those demolished was the porticoed Georgian house at No. 85 High Street; it was replaced in the 1980s by a row of shops. It was here, in 1812, that the novelist Anna Porter watched her neighbour, as she thought, walk into her house looking agitated and upset only to stalk out again seconds later. A maid was sent to the man's house to ask him what the problem was, only to discover that he had dropped dead of a stroke at the precise moment that Miss Porter had seen his apparition.

Claremont House

Standing off the Portsmouth Road south-west of Esher is the grand Claremont House. This magnificent Palladian mansion was built in the 1770s by Robert Clive, better known as Clive of India, on the site of an earlier house that was the English

The grand Claremont House just south of Esher is host to the ghost of one of England's finest architects, though one who came to a sad end here.

Cobham Park House stands in extensive grounds and is private property. That does not matter overmuch, as the ghost has been seen in nearby lanes as well as around the house.

seat of the Irish Earl of Clare. The house was first called Clare Mount, but by Clive's day had become known as Claremont. The house is now a public school, but the grounds are open to the public and it is here that the ghost is seen.

The phantom is that of an elderly man dressed in a long dark overcoat or cloak. He is seen most often near the lake. This ghost is usually identified as the great architect William Kent. Kent was hired by the Clare family to rework the grounds, with the artificial lake and island as its centrepiece. Kent and the Clare argued repeatedly over the design and in the end Kent was sacked. He presented the Clares with a bill for £200 - then a huge sum. The earl offered £100, but Kent flew into a temper, causing the earl to have him thrown off the estate. A week later Kent was back, this time carrying two loaded pistols. The earl called for two burly servants who proceeded to beat up the architect and throw him into the lake that he had created. Kent suffered a collapse, fell ill of a fever and was dead within ten days. No wonder his mournful ghost returns to pace about the lakeside.

Cobham

Continuing past Claremont, the old Portsmouth Road crosses the modern A3 then drops down into the village of Cobham. Just on the left is a modern healthcare centre. When I was a boy there was a pub here called the Tartar.

Motorists used to be waved down on rainy evenings by a young woman hitching a lift. If the driver stopped, the woman would get in without a word and point down the hill towards the village centre. When the motorist reached the village, the woman would vanish into thin air – giving the unfortunate motorist a shock. Who the ghostly hitchhiker might have been is unknown, though she was first reported in 1947. It is perhaps just as well that she has not been seen since the pub was pulled down.

If you leave Cobham on the lane towards Downside you will pass on your left the grand old mansion of Cobham Park. This fine house was built for John Ligonier when he retired from the army in 1766 loaded down with honours, having been created a Field Marshal and a Knight of the Bath - not bad for an almost penniless Protestant refugee from France who had joined the army to avoid starvation. Although he was one of the most senior and highly regarded officers in the British Army, Ligonier chose to spend his retirement in debauchery. He threw many drunken parties for his office pals and seduced a succession of local girls, adding extensions to Cobham Park as apartments for the women and their children.

John Ligonier, whose phantom walks the area south of Cobham, was an extraordinary character. Born in France, he joined the British Army to fight the French and fought at battles as famous as Blenheim, Ramillies, Oudenard and Malplaquet – where he caught the eye of the Duke of Marlborough by ending the day with twenty-three bullet holes in his clothing, but no serious injury to his body.

He kept fit by going for long walks along the banks of the River Mole around Cobham, Downside and Stoke D'Abernon. It is here that his ghost has been seen, striking about in his old military greatcoat.

Back in Cobham itself, St Andrew's Church is a pretty structure that can boast some impressively large tombstones in the churchyard. During the 1960s and '70s the churchyard also boasted a spectral donkey, that was made even more unusual by being blue. It was first seen by the bell-ringers as they left the church after an evening practice session.

The oldest parts of the Church of St Andrew in Cobham are some 850 years old, and every century since has seen some sort of work or other carried out here. Quite when the churchyard picked up its unique phantom is unclear.

The bridge over the River Mole west of Cobham was built to carry the main London to Portsmouth Road, the A3. In the 1970s the bridge was bypassed by the Esher Bypass, which carried the A3 around Cobham as well. The ghost, however, prefers to stick to the old bridge.

West of Cobham, the Portsmouth Road crosses the Mole by way of a twentieth-century bridge that replaced a succession of wooden structures. It is on this bridge that the apparition of a man in a long black overcoat has been seen. It is not the coat that makes most impression on witnesses, but the hideous ugliness of the man's face. It is quite unnerving, apparently.

Walton-on-Thames

Running north from Cobham is the Seven Hills Road, which is haunted by an elderly woman in a grey coat who has the unnerving habit of stepping out in front of cars. The road leads to Walton-on-Thames, a town which was massively redeveloped

in the twentieth century as the railway encouraged commuting into London, with a consequent growth in house building. There are vestiges of the pre-railway Walton to be found, and the most significant is the Walton Manor, tucked away down the aptly named Manor Road overlooking the Thames.

The timber-framed house was built in the fourteenth century, was altered with each passing century, and has recently undergone restoration. The ghost to be met here is that of an elderly man in sombre black clothes. Tradition has it that this is John Bradshaw, a hugely successful lawyer who lived here in the seventeenth century. Rich and famous as he was for his legal career, it was in 1649 that Bradshaw took on the task that earned him enduring fame and which

The Oatlands Hotel just outside Weybridge perpetuates the name of the Tudor hunting lodge beloved of King Henry VIII. The current building, like the ghost sometimes seen here, dates back only to the nineteenth century.

has, apparently, led to the haunting. He was asked by Oliver Cromwell to be the presiding judge at the trial of King Charles I. Bradshaw was reluctant to take on the role as he had doubts about the legality of the trial, and about his own safety. Throughout the trial he wore armour under his judicial robes and a specially made hat that hid bullet-proof steel under the felt crown. He survived the trial and went on to reap the rewards, gaining important and lucrative positions under the Cromwellian government that followed on the king's execution.

Bradshaw died of a fever in 1659, which was probably just as well. The following year the executed king's son returned to the throne as Charles II and ordered the imprisonment or execution of those involved in his father's trial. Bradshaw did

not escape, despite being already dead. His body was exhumed, beheaded and hung in chains at Tyburn before being thrown into an unmarked pit. From there the bones were rescued by Bradshaw's son who fled the kingdom to Jamaica, where he had them interred on Gun Hill under a tablet that is still to be seen.

Whether Bradshaw's ghost returns to his old home due to an uneasy conscience over his role in the execution of a king or because of the way his body was treated nobody really knows.

Weybridge

Three miles upstream along the Thames from Walton lies Weybridge. Just east of the town centre is a glorious late eighteenth-century mansion, now the Oatlands Park Hotel. This house occupies the site of the Tudor Oatlands Palace, a much-loved hunting lodge of Henry VIII. The palace fell into ruin, and was cleared in 1790 for a new house built by Prince Frederick, the Duke of York of nursery rhyme fame. Among the many guests was the famous dandy Beau Brummell, who is rumoured to have had an affair with the duchess. This house forms the core of the present hotel, though it was remodelled in 1865 and again in the twentieth century. The phantom woman seen on the second floor is said to be a serving girl who worked here in the later nineteenth century. She had a furious row with her boyfriend one evening, came back in tears and threw herself out of her window to her death.

The grounds of Oatlands House were famous for the grotto built at great expense by the Duchess of Newcastle who lived here before the Yorks. The grotto was lost when the extensive grounds were sold off for housing, but before it went it gave its name to the Grotto Inn which still stands on Monument Hill. This was originally the laundry house for the Tudor house. There is a blocked-up passage down in the cellar that is rumoured to lead to Oatlands. From the passage have been heard footsteps accompanied by the most unearthly spectral moans and groans – leading to speculation about what might be found if the passage is ever opened up. So far nobody has had the courage.

Upstairs in the main pub there are two ghosts that are seen often. These are both children, a boy and a girl. The barman

The Grotto Pub in Weybridge takes its name from the folly, in the shape of a cave fitted with statues, a waterfall and imitation stalactites. The pub is very welcoming, though rather less ornate, and the ghosts seem to enjoy it here.

A de Havilland DH 82 Tiger Moth from the 1930s. It was one of these aircraft that crashed tragically at Brooklands, leaving behind a phantom spectacle that is sometimes seen in the skies over Weybridge.

tells me that he sees them once or twice a month and that they seem quite happy little souls as they run about playing some game of their own. A barmaid once got a very clear view of them in an upstairs room. She said that they looked as if they were wearing clothes from the eighteenth century and agreed that they gave every appearance of being quite cheerful.

One odd occurrence at the grotto that does not seem to be linked to the two children, at least no connection is obvious, came in June 2010. A guest was sitting up reading in bed when he happened to glance across the room to see a fireplace that he did not recall noticing when he had entered the room. He looked at it for some seconds, noting its Victorian cast-iron surround and tiles. Then he returned to his book. When he looked up again the fireplace had gone.

An unusual phantom lurks not so much in Weybridge as over it. In 1934 or thereabouts, a single-seater biplane was flying over the town when it ran into a sudden storm. The light aircraft was thrown about by the turbulent winds, the pilot lost control and the plane crashed – with fatal consequences. On similarly stormy days the apparition of the doomed aircraft has been seen and heard over the town.

The pilot was making for Brooklands, a mile or so south-west of the town, then the home of a leading private air club and motor-racing circuit. Both air club and racing club have long since gone, but the air club HQ, hangars and workshops remain. They now house an air museum that boasts not only a Concorde but also the only intact Wellington in the country and dozens of other aircraft. There are also long sections of the massively banked motor-racing track and it is these that are haunted.

Opened in 1907 as the world's first purpose-built motor sport venue, Brooklands had an oval track almost 3 miles long, a hill climb course and extensive pit facilities. The track quickly became a venue for races, testing and record attempts. On 31 October 1913, Percy 'Pearly' Lambert came to Brooklands with his purpose-built Talbot speed car to try to regain the world speed record. He had been the first man to travel at 100mph, but a French man named Jean Chassagne had since reached 107mph. The track was cleared of any possible debris, the Talbot tweaked to perfection and Lambert got a good night's sleep. Everything was ready.

At 9.20 a.m. Lambert set off. The officials watching timed his twentieth lap at 110.4mph and began celebrating, but then tragedy struck. As Lambert came around one of the banked curves a tyre burst. He was seen to apply the brakes and to keep the car on a straight course, but then he lost control. The car flipped over and cartwheeled several times before coming to rest in a mangled wreck. Lambert was dead.

The haunting began soon after. The figure of Lambert as he was on that fatal day, complete with leather overalls and tight leather cap, was seen wandering about the pits and in the area of track where he died. The most recent firm sighting was in the 1970s, but the area is still said to be haunted and local people

A section of the old track at Brooklands racing circuit together with the remains of the pits. It was not far from here that racing driver Percy Lambert was killed in 1913. His ghost returns still.

have reported seeing and hearing odd things into the twenty-first century.

Chertsey

Further upstream along the Thames lies the town of Chertsey. For centuries this was famous for its abbey, founded in 666 by St Erkenwald, later Bishop of London, which came to own most of north-western Surrey. It was closed by King Henry VIII in 1537 and only scant ruins remain today. Many archaeological finds from the abbey have made their way to the Chertsey Museum in Windsor Street (though the famous moulded tiles depicting the tale of Tristan and Iseult were taken by the British Museum). It is in the Chertsey Museum that the first of Chertsey's spectres can be found. The museum opened to the public in 1965 in a grand old porticoed house that had formerly been a doctor's surgery and home combined.

The sound of a child running about has frequently been reported here. What makes this ghost interesting is that the footsteps are quite clearly those of a small child scampering about on a hard floor – most people say a wooden floor – although the rooms in which it is heard are carpeted. This is an often remarked upon feature of ghosts, that they behave as if they are still experiencing the property as it was when they were alive, not as it is now. In this case the child is running about on the polished wooden floors of a bygone era. Other ghosts walk through bricked-up doorways, or stride along floors that no longer exist, and so seem to float in mid air, or gaze out of windows that are now bricked up.

This behaviour is typical of what are often termed 'classic ghosts', those phantoms which make up the vast majority of reported hauntings. These ghosts repeat the same behaviour every time they are seen, paying no attention to the humans who encounter them nor to any changes made to the building they haunt. If the ghost walks down a staircase once, it will walk down it every time – even if the stairs are no longer there.

This has led some researchers to postulate that ghosts are some form of psychic recording of a past event. Known as the 'stone tape theory', the suggestion is that the stones, bricks or wood of a building somehow capture a recording of an event, akin to a DVD, that is then played back under certain conditions to be seen by whoever is present. Another theory to account for these classic ghosts is that they are, in fact, a crack in time. For some reason, it is suggested, an event will open up a break into the future. Anybody who is in the right place at that point in the future is able to peer back in time to see a glimpse of the past - which they interpret as seeing a ghost.

Like Weybridge, Chertsey expanded greatly in the twentieth century, engulfing the surrounding farmlands in housing estates. One of the few rural survivors is the Golden Grove Inn, a 400-year-old country tavern that stands at the foot of St Ann's Hill to the north-west of the town centre. The pub is haunted by a rather indistinct female phantom which appears quite regularly in an upstairs room.

Without any real evidence, a story has grown up that links this phantom to the vanished abbey. Apparently one of the monks at the abbey was considerably less holy than he should have been. In the medieval period this was not as unusual as might be thought. Many younger sons were enrolled into the Church as the lands were earmarked for the elder son. Other men joined the Church in search

The museum at Chertsey has fine displays linked to the town's history, but the ghost here seems to date back to the days when this was a private house.

The Golden Grove pub near Chertsey is justifiably proud of its food, but it is a centuries old murder that led to the haunting here.

The ancient phantom of the King's Head in Chertsey boasts a feature rather unusual among phantoms – he trails a smell in his wake that is quite distinctive.

Golden Grove. The girl was pretty, flirtatious even, and the monk became obsessed. The girl, however, was wisely saving herself for a good marriage prospect and spurned the monk's advances. So he came back one night to rape her; he then killed her and hid her body. The murder was soon discovered and the monk quickly identified as the prime suspect.

As a monk, he could plead 'benefit of clergy', which meant that his crime was tried in an ecclesiastical court, not in a royal court. Although his guilt was never in doubt, the ecclesiastical court acted with customary leniency. They did not execute anyone, no matter what the crime, and usually ordered criminal clergy to undergo a penance, pilgrimage or other punishment. Understandably, the victims of crimes committed by clergy were unimpressed and abuses of the system did much to promote the Reformation that saw the rise of Protestantism and the fall of great abbeys such as Chertsey.

What happened to the killer monk of Chertsey, tradition does not say. But the poor girl returned to her old home in spectral form. Unfortunately for the story, the Golden Grove was built about sixty years after Chertsey Abbey was closed down. That is not to say, of course, that there was not an earlier inn on the site, so perhaps there is some truth in the tale after all.

Another spectral relic of the great abbey is to be found in the King's Head in Guildford Street. Here it is a monk that does the haunting, not his victim. The monk in question has no story explaining his haunting, but he appears quite often and sometimes leaves an unpleasant smell in his wake. He walks in all areas of the pub, but his most spectacular appearance came upstairs in 1977. An Australian barmaid was asleep in her room when the bedclothes

of a steady career with lucrative prospects. Such men were looking for personal advancement rather than sacred devotions. Inevitably they had an interest in hunting, gambling, feasting, drink and women every bit as lively as did their secular counterparts. On the whole, society was tolerant of such men, so long as they performed their religious duties and did not stray too far from moral behaviour.

This particular monk, however, was altogether worse. He was in the habit of drinking in taverns near the abbey, as were others, and it was on one such visit that he met the daughter of the landlord of the were tugged violently off her bed, bringing her to wakefulness with a shock. Glaring at her from the darkness was the phantom monk. Understandably the poor girl fled into the night to seek safety with a friend who lived not far away. She never went back, not even to collect her belongings, and sent her friend to collect her wages and clothes. The ghostly monk is said to be linked to a priest hole, so maybe he is a Catholic priest from the decades after the abbey closed rather than an actual monk.

A priest hole – or rather holes, as there are two of them – is to be found at the George, also in Guildford Street. This pub began life as a fourteenth-century hunting lodge before becoming an inn a couple of centuries later. The ghost here is usually said to be a grey lady, though since nobody is on record as having seen it this must remain in doubt. The ghost does, however, seem to be female as the footsteps that are heard so often moving about upstairs are dainty and seem to have a high heel. A few guests have reported feeling that somebody has sat down on the bed that they are in, and rather more report that furniture is moved about by unseen hands.

Addlestone

South of Chertsey lies the village of Addlestone. As with so many places in

The Crouch Oak at Addlestone is a famous local landmark, being one of the oldest trees in England. The ghost materialises here and then walks towards the church where it vanishes. (Courtesy of 80N)

Surrey, Addlestone grew massively after the railway came, but there are some ancient survivals. The villagers are most proud of the Crouch Oak, a massive tree estimated to be at least 900 years old that stands in the High Street. In medieval times the tree marked the boundary of Windsor Forest, the hunting grounds used by the king when in residence at Windsor Castle. That forest survives in part as Windsor Great Park. Queen Elizabeth I had a picnic under the tree and it has long been a focus for public meetings and religious sermons.

The ghostly lady of Addlestone was for many years said to walk from the Crouch Oak to St Paul's Church in nearby Church Road. She is said to wear a long, dark-coloured dress that rustles audibly as she walks with bowed head. She is traditionally said to be a local young woman who went mad with despair after being jilted by a heartless lover. Her date is variously put at anywhere between the 1820s and 1910s, so this may be a later legend invented to explain the haunting.

The most famous sighting of the ghost came in October 1953 when the local policeman, PC Battams, was walking his usual night patrol around the village centre. He had just come out of School Lane into Church Road when something made him stop and look about him. He distinctly heard footsteps coming from the church, but could see nothing. Moving back into School Lane, Battams caught a glimpse of a woman in a long grey coat, but she vanished before he could catch up with her.

In 2004 an unknown arsonist set fire to both the tree and the church. The oak survived, but the church went up in flames. The church has since been rebuilt, but so far as I can tell there has been no sighting of the phantom lady since the fires.

Virginia Water

A few miles west of Addlestone, up the Bourne Stream that is one of the smaller tributaries of the Thames, lies the famously affluent village of Virginia Water. The village takes its name from the vast artificial lake to the west which was formed in 1746 when the Bourne was dammed by order of William, Duke of Cumberland, the son of King George III who was then in residence at Windsor Castle. The lake is famed in fishing circles as the place where Britain's largest pike, a monster of 55lb, was caught, but it is better known in recent years as the venue for the filming of lakeside scenes in the Harry Potter movies.

Overlooking the lake is the Wheatsheaf Hotel on London Road. The story behind this haunting began at the Sloane Square branch of a national bank on the afternoon of 1 December 1949. An off duty policeman, Superintendent Robert Lee, was walking past when he saw a man he recognised entering the bank carrying a very large package wrapped up in brown paper. The man, Lee knew, was Barry Fieldsen, a petty crook who had served time a dozen years earlier for fencing stolen goods, but who had since then evaded conviction though he was known still to be involved with the underworld. Lee wondered what a man like Fieldsen could be doing at such a prestigious bank and just how he had managed to afford the expensively tailored suit that he was wearing.

Lee loitered long enough to see Fieldsen leave without the package, then he slipped into the bank to ask questions. The manager told him that the client was an ex-army officer named Redvers Holliday who had a strong box in the bank in which he regularly deposited and retrieved assorted packages, all of which were sealed closed.

The lake at Virginia Water attracted a notorious London crook in 1950, though he was to come to a violent end that has led to a haunting. (Courtesy of SuzanneKn)

Lee soon discovered that Major Redvers Holliday had been killed in the recently ended war and that Fieldsen had used documents stolen from his widow three years earlier to obtain the strongbox. That was enough to get a search warrant. The strongbox turned out to contain a massively valuable collection of jewels, silverware and other valuables. Most were identified as having been stolen from the rich and powerful by a consummate conman who went by many names, but was known at Scotland Yard as 'Gentleman Johnny'. He would work his way into the confidence of a victim, get himself an invitation to their house and then spirit away any jewels or other valuables he could find.

Fieldsen was arrested and charged with receiving stolen goods while Lee and his team set to work trying to prove a link between Fieldsen and the elusive Gentleman Johnny. On 14 December, Fieldsen put up the £3,000 bail demanded and walked free. On 22 December Lee took a phone call that brought him to the Wheatsheaf Hotel at Virginia Water. A regular client by the name of Dudley Ednam had shot himself dead in Room 23. Ednam was none other than Fieldsen under yet another alias. He had left a note saying 'I hope I am not causing you too much trouble'. It soon transpired that Fieldsen was not just the fence selling Johnny the Gent's hauls, but he was Johnny the Gent himself.

Since then the dark figure sometimes seen lurking upstairs has been assumed to be this master criminal.

Unusually, the Wheatsheaf has, or rather had, a second phantom. Back in the 1930s, a guest here was a London barrister who preferred to keep his name secret, although his story was widely reported at the time. This man was staying at the Wheatsheaf while visiting a wealthy client who lived nearby on some complex business that was taking several days. One evening he was sitting in the main bar, smoking a pipe after dinner, when he saw an apparition of an old friend. He had been at school with this friend and although they had been very close then, they had drifted apart and had not spoken for some years. His friend, the man thought, worked in some importation business. The apparition was joined by a second, that of a man wearing Indian dress. The two men began arguing, though no sound could be heard. Then the second man whipped out a knife and stabbed the friend in the chest – whereupon the vision faded.

Understandably shaken, the barrister noted the event and promised himself that when he got home he would send a letter to his old friend to tell him about the incident. He did not have time. When he returned home the barrister found a telegram advising him that his friend had been killed in India and that a memorial service would be held shortly. It transpired that the friend had been stabbed in the chest during an altercation on a railway train with a client in India – and that the killer matched the description of the apparition seen by the barrister at the Wheatsheaf in Virginia Water.

The house on Egham Hill that was once the subject of a protracted court case in which the resident ghost took centre stage. The building is now divided up into flats and the phantom is seen no more.

Egham

North from Virginia Water lies Egham, about as far north as it is possible to go in Surrey, for the Thames makes a bend here before looping away into Berkshire. In 1903 a large house here hit the news headlines due to a haunting by a ghost that became as famous as any ghost could be. At the bottom of Egham Hill, where the road from the south-west becomes the High Street, stood a fine Italianate villa by the name of Hillside. In 1903 the then owner, Charles Barret, moved out and rented the grand house to a Mr Stephen Phillips on a year's rent of £70, paid in advance. Less than a month later Philips moved out, claiming that the house was haunted. He asked for his rent back, but Barret refused and put the house up for rent again.

There the matter may have rested, except that Phillips was an actor whose poetry was highly regarded and who was well

connected in fashionable society in London. He soon told his tale, which became widely known in London. The haunting had begun soon after Phillips and his family moved in. It had started with the sounds of footsteps and whispering. Soon doors would open and close themselves. Phillips' four-year-old daughter then began saying that there was a nasty man who would stare at her whenever she was left alone in a room. This prompted Phillips to ask the locals if the house was haunted. They told him that it was not, but that before Hillside had been built in the 1880s the site had belonged to a farm in which lived a farmer with an evil reputation as a drunkard and wife beater. The farmer's young daughter had died many years earlier and gossip had it that he had beaten her to death in a drunken temper. Fearing for the safety of his own daughter at the hands of the phantom 'nasty man', Phillips had moved out.

The story came to the ears of the *Daily Express* and *Daily Mail*. Both newspapers printed an account of the dramatic events and although neither paper gave the address, the *Express'* story contained enough details for locals in Egham to know which house was the subject of the story. Phillips found it impossible to rent out the property and decided to sue the two newspapers for his loss of income. The *Express* settled out of court – they were thought to have paid £200 – but the *Mail* chose to fight the action.

When the case came to court it caused a sensation. Everyone was expecting to hear dramatic details of the haunting and see London's most eminent lawyers arguing with each other over ghosts. The *Mail* was defending the case on the grounds that ghosts did not exist and so no landlord could lose money because of them. But when the action began the presiding judge began by ruling that the existence or otherwise of ghosts was immaterial to the case and ruled as inadmissible all the *Mail's* evidence. Instead, he said, the only real point at issue was whether Phillips had failed to rent the property because potential lessees believed it to be haunted as a result of the story in the *Mail*. Unsurprisingly, Barret won his case and was awarded £100 damages plus costs.

The *Mail*, however, appealed. They brought forward witnesses who testified that the real reason the house could not be let was that the advent of the motor car had made the steep hill a very noisy and fume-ridden place in which to live. A procession of would-be lessees explained the problems, and stated that while the rent asked by Mr Phillips would have been reasonable ten years earlier, when only horses went by, the combination of motorised transport and the steep hill made it unreasonable. The *Mail* won their appeal.

Hillside villa is still there, though it has now been divided up into flats. It now overlooks the A30, the main road out of London up the Thames Valley and the motorised traffic is heavy and continuous. One wonders what the people of 1903 would make of it today. The ghost seems to have made up his mind. He has not been reported for years.

Englefield Green

Just west along the A30 is Englefield Green, a pretty place dominated by the Royal Holloway College to the south and Runnymede Meadows – where King John signed the Magna Carta – to the north. Overlooking the village green, where cricket is played on summer weekends, is the Barley Mow. Although the ghost is to be found in the pub, the story behind the haunting begins at a house just round the corner in Jude's Hill. In October 1852 this was the home of the village doctor. One morning, before he had even arrived at the breakfast table, the doctor was summoned by a highly agitated Frenchmen. The Frenchman rode with the doctor north of the village to Priest Hill. There he found another Frenchman with a bullet wound in his chest and four other Frenchmen standing around waiting.

As soon as the doctor arrived the four Frenchmen fled, heading towards Egham station to return to London. Having sent the remaining Frenchman to get help, the doctor tended the wounded man. He then sent a passing local to run to Egham station to send a telegram to Scotland Yard asking them to arrest the Frenchmen heading for London. The wounded man was carried to the Barley Mow, where he lingered in great pain for some hours before he died.

It transpired that the dead man was a French army officer named Frederic Courmet who had pronounced republican views and so had fled into exile when Emperor Napoleon III had come to power the previous year. The killer was another exile, Emmanuel Barthelemy, who claimed to be a staunch republican but who was suspected of being a secret agent of Napoleon. The two men had argued over a woman, claimed by Barthelemy to be his fiancée, and this had led to a duel.

By 1852 duelling was illegal in Britain, and any death that resulted was deemed to be murder. All five surviving Frenchmen were charged with murder and brought to trial. The exiles maintained that they had not known duelling to be illegal, that the dead Courmet had been a willing participant and that the death could not be considered to be murder. The jury agreed and convicted Barthelemy of manslaughter, acquitting the rest. Barthelemy was later released, only to be hanged some years later for an unrelated murder.

The unfortunate Courmet had meanwhile been buried in Egham church. His funeral was attended by hundreds of French exiles and was the most dramatic funeral the town had ever seen. Back at the Barley Mow his ghost began to walk. These days his phantom is more likely to be heard than seen – the sounds of hideous gasping and moaning of a man in great pain being heard. And a most unnerving sound it is too.

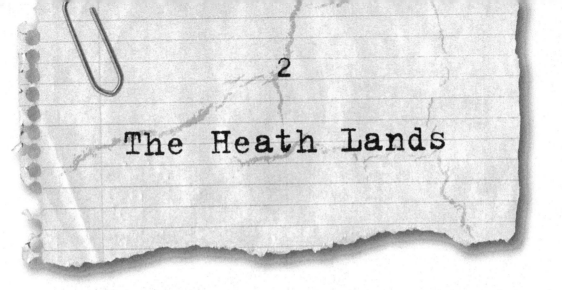

2

The Heath Lands

SQUEEZED between the Thames and the Downs at the western end of Surrey is a section of sandy heath lands that stretch west into Berkshire and Hampshire. The little town of Frimley lies right on the edge of Surrey, and the Hampshire border runs along the Blackwater River at the end of Frimley High Street.

Frimley

Standing in the middle of the High Street is Ye Olde White Hart. The pub name comes from the badge of King Richard II, who was overthrown and murdered by his cousin (who thus became King Henry IV). Those remaining loyal to Richard showed their feelings by using a white hart badge on their homes and businesses. At the time, Frimley was a small village owned by the mighty Chertsey Abbey, so it is odd that they allowed this display of hostility to the king. Be that as it may, the oldest of the pub's three ghosts dates back to this period.

Local legend has it that the inn was used by the more worldly monks of Chertsey to do their drinking and womanising at a safe distance from the watchful eyes of their abbot. One monk found himself getting rather heavily involved with an attractive young woman whom he met regularly at the inn, consummating their relationship in an upstairs room. Nobody seemed to know much about this woman, other than that she was not a local, but she spent freely enough.

The feelings of the monk, landlord and others involved can best be imagined when a group of armed men burst into the pub one day as the monk was enjoying the woman's company upstairs. It turned out that the woman was a nun who had been systematically pilfering the convent's treasury and spending the cash on loose living. The men had followed her to the inn to arrest her and drag her off for her crimes. They burst in on the monk and nun with swords drawn, but the nun did not intend to be caught so easily and leapt out of the window. In the struggle that ensued, the monk was injured and the nun killed.

It is the ghost of this luckless nun which comes back to haunt the upstairs bar and adjacent areas of Ye Olde White Hart. She has been seen dressed in a long grey gown – presumably her habit – and since the pub gained electric power has taken to

The Olde White Hart, Frimley, can lay claim to no fewer than three ghosts, each coming from a different century of the inn's long and prosperous history.

switching lights on and off in the rooms she haunts.

The second ghost in this pub haunts the bar that was formerly the stables. Back in Georgian days the stables were the preserve of the head ostler, who managed the stables, providing care for the guests' horses and ensuring that there was always a change of fresh horses for the stagecoaches that called here on their journeys from London to Portsmouth and back. The service was highly efficient and the ostler picked up good tips from the naval officers dashing up and down the Portsmouth Road on naval business. He had several men to keep the system running and prided himself on always looking smartly turned out in his spotless white frock coat and high leather riding boots.

So far as anyone could tell, the ostler had a good and prosperous living. But something must have been wrong, for he hanged himself from a beam in the stables one night. The figure of a burly man in a white coat has been seen often in this part of the pub.

The third phantom of the pub is more elusive. He is said to have been a Chinese man who worked in the kitchens and who was killed in a brawl. However, his phantom has not been seen recently and details are vague.

Rather better known is the phantom of Old Charlie Miles. Miles was a retired colonel who lived in Frimley and regularly took his dog for a walk on the common. Miles usually wore his leather jacket and deer-

The sinful life of the errant monk of Frimley came to a violent end at Ye Olde White Hart, but it is the ghost of his lover, not of he himself, that has been reported here.

stalker hat. He died in 1957, but since then he has returned in spectral form to walk his equally phantom dog up the Old Guildford Road that leads south of the town to reach the common.

Pirbright

East of Frimley at Pirbright is to be found another haunted White Hart pub. The ghost here is that of a tall man dressed in black and wearing a hat. He is seen upstairs in a part of the pub not generally open to the public.

Send

Further east again is the village of Send, where the historic Boughton Hall has been converted into a care home for the elderly. The ghost here is of an elderly man smoking a pipe who potters about the grounds and upstairs. I am told that the smell of his pungent tobacco has been noticed more often than he is seen himself.

Newark Priory

North from Send, the lane to Pyrford crosses the River Wey at Newark Bridge, a narrow humpbacked affair. Visible across the meadows to the east are the ruins of Newark Priory. This holy house was founded in the twelfth century by local landowner Rauld de Calva, who dedicated it to the Virgin Mary. The priory managed to lead an entirely uneventful existence until, along with all other religious houses, it was closed down by orders of King Henry VIII during the sixteenth-century Reformation. Like most other monasteries, Newark Priory was stripped of anything of value – including the windows, lead roofs and decorative stonework – leaving only the bare walls. Uniquely, however, Newark Priory was then used for target practice by a battery of the king's artillery. Firing from a position close to Pyrford church, the guns reduced the priory to the ruined condition in which it stands.

The guns did not, however, drive away the ghosts. The shades of several monks have been seen pottering about the old ruins or walking along the banks of the Wey. According to local tradition, some of the monks drowned in the river. One of the monks appeared inside the vicarage at Pyrford in the 1930s, but he was seen only once and does not seem to have returned.

The ruins of Newark Priory at Pyrford. Along with all monasteries in England, Newark was closed down on the order of King Henry VIII, though the monarch could do nothing about the phantom monks that remain there to this day.

Horsell

To the north-west lies Horsell. Once a village in its own right, it has since been swallowed up by the housing splurge that grew up around Woking railway station. Church Hill runs from the High Street down to Brewery Road and the canal. An old friend of mine who lives here tells me that a ghostly carriage pulls up outside the church, waits for a few minutes and then sets off down the hill. Apparently it is heading for the railway station, though nobody seems to have seen it once it gets beyond the bottom of the hill. Presumably it is invisible beyond that point.

According to one version of this tale the coach is pulled by four headless horses. This macabre touch is often associated with tales of evil men, wicked deeds or even of the Devil himself. Perhaps this particular phantom coach was originally linked to some terrible deed of times gone by. If so, the act has been forgotten. The coach may be a local manifestation of the Death Coach, a gruesome phantom that is reported mostly from western England, Wales and Ireland. The Death Coach is said to herald an imminent death in the village where it appears, and sometimes that it has been sent by the Devil to collect a wicked soul that has been earmarked for Hell.

North and east of Horsell stretch are the extensive woodlands of Horsell Common, through which flows the boggy stream known as Danewell Gutter.

The Church of St Mary in Horsell is of twelfth-century origin, though most of the current building dates to the fourteenth century. A sinister coach is said to pull up outside the lych gate as if waiting for a passenger; it then sets off down the hill towards Woking.

The ghost of Ripley's Talbot Inn has not been seen
since a recent and most impressive refurbishment
was completed – at least, not so far.

Along the banks of this little water course has been seen a ghostly man carrying a rucksack. Who he might be and why he haunts this comparatively obscure spot are unknown.

Ripley

To the south-east lies the lovely village of Ripley, so much quieter now that the busy A3 bypasses the village entirely. One of the most impressive buildings in the High Street is the Talbot Inn. This is perhaps the finest coaching inn in Surrey, complete with towering archway through which the stagecoaches of yesteryear could pass to the yard and stables behind. The façade is all elegant Georgian brickwork, complete with ornamental arched windows, but this is a mere pretence for the building behind is much older, being made up of sixteenth-century timber and wattle.

The ghost here is that of a coachman. He was not, apparently, one of the drivers who called here but a local Ripley man who worked at the inn welcoming guests who popped in for a meal or drink while the horses were changed. He seems to have been in charge of the coach yard and all that went on there. However, he was also a heavy drinker – and one night he drank too much. The unfortunate man took a tumble down the stairs and died.

The inn has recently been refurbished to a very high standard. The manager told me that the ghostly coachman has not been seen since the work was completed. Whether he has been driven out or is merely taking a break remains to be seen.

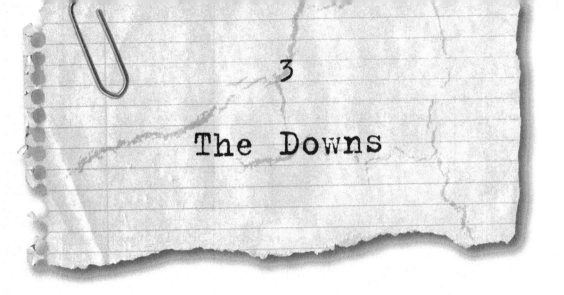

3

The Downs

THE sweeping chalk downs dominate central Surrey. In the west they are neither so tall nor as precipitous as they are to the east, but they remain impressive enough. The Downs have long had a character unique to themselves. The thin, upland soil is not suited to agriculture but it does make for fine sheep pasture. For centuries, sheep was the main business on these hills – Surrey wool was counted among the finest in southern England. Shepherds and sheep apart, these were lonely places. Travellers preferred to keep to the valleys, as they offered easy access from north to south. The exception was the Pilgrim's Way, a prehistoric track that skirted along the southern edge of the Downs. In medieval times it was used by pilgrims moving between Winchester and Canterbury Cathedrals, which is how it got its name, but it was much older than that in origin.

The Pilgrim's Way

Between Farnham and Guildford the old track ran along a long, narrow chalk ridge known locally as the Hog's Back due to its shape. The route along the Hog's Back is today occupied by the A31 dual carriageway. The North Downs Way, a long-distance footpath that in many places follows the Pilgrims Way, runs along the southern face of the ridge.

About halfway along the Hog's Back, close to where the A31 passes a disused quarry, a phantom horse-drawn carriage has been seen. The carriage appears only at night and most witnesses report that a dim lantern gleams from its front. Descriptions of the vehicle vary, as might be expected of a ghostly object seen only at night. It would, however, seem to be high sided and the driver sits perched up on a box seat. It most recently made the local news headlines with a sighting in January 2007.

Rather more dramatic, and mysterious, was the ghost car that was seen on the A3 just the other side of Guildford on the evening of 11 December 2002. Several motorists pulled over to call police on their mobile phones when a car was seen to veer suddenly off the road at high speed and smash into a patch of densely wooded undergrowth. Two of the motorists waited long enough for the police to turn up so that they could give their names. The police

A car crash on the A3 at Merrow in 2002 saw the police called in to investigate an apparition that proved beyond their powers to solve.

then began a search, though there were no signs of a car having left the road.

After a few minutes probing the undergrowth, the police found a crashed Vauxhall Astra car. It was nose down in a ditch, covered in brambles and invisible from the road. More mysterious still was the fact that the car had obviously been there for some months. Inside was the body of the driver, reduced almost to a skeleton. A police spokesman later said: 'We believe the car left the road and ended up in the ditch during July. It doesn't appear that any other vehicles were involved. The car was discovered as a result of a report from members of the public who thought they saw a car's headlights veering off the road.' The driver was later identified from dental records.

One officer called the discovery of the five-month old corpse 'spine-chilling', and the motorists who reported the incident have been left wondering whether they saw a ghostly re-enactment of the original crash.

Merrow

Up on the Downs south of Burpham and the A3 is the village of Merrow, which has managed to retain something of its own character despite being virtually swallowed by the expanding suburbs of Guildford. In 1977 the village hit first the local, and then the national, news headlines when a poltergeist visitation occurred in a home on Finches Rise.

The poltergeist of Merrow hit the national headlines in 1977 and at the time was blamed on the spirit of an eighteenth-century murderer – but things were not that simple.

Poltergeists are quite different from the more usual ghost. They are rarely seen, but they are the stuff of nightmares. They can throw objects about with force, start fires, write obscene or threatening messages, smash furniture and destroy valued objects of all kinds. The mayhem usually lasts a few weeks, sometimes months, and then ends as mysteriously as it began. In this particular case the poltergeist specialised in hiding watches, keys and other small objects as well as throwing them about. It also created sudden chills in the house and was capable of pinning people down in bed or snatching at their clothes.

Once the story was in the local press, a historian found that almost exactly 200 years before the trouble began three men had been hanged for armed highway robbery – mugging, as we would call it today

– on a scaffold erected just a few yards from where the affected house was later built. It was assumed at the time that the poltergeist was caused by the unquiet spirit of one of the dead men, but poltergeists are not so easily explained as that. In any case, the ghostly goings-on soon faded, and then ceased.

Clandon House

Rather more long lived has been the phantom lady of Clandon House, which stands in Clandon Park beside West Clandon. The clearest sighting of this ghost came in 1896 when a house party of almost twenty people were visiting William, 4th Earl Onslow, whose seat this was. The guests were returning to the house after a day's shooting on the earl's extensive estates when they saw, striding across the lawns, a woman dressed in a long cream dress. What really drew their attention, however, was that the woman was brandishing a large hunting knife and weeping desperately. No sooner had this startling apparition been seen than she promptly vanished. The witnesses who had seen the phantom soon agreed that the figure had resembled Lady Elizabeth Onslow, an unmarried daughter of the family who had died some years earlier. There had been some rumours that Lady Elizabeth had been mentally disturbed – which might explain the behaviour of her phantom.

The lady in cream with the knife has been seen several times since her dramatic debut. She is said to have once walked up the steps, through the front door and across the famous Marble Hall before vanishing. More often she is seen in the grounds, wandering about waving her knife over her head.

Seen much less often in the grounds is the ghost of a man sporting a luxuriant beard. He is sometimes accompanied by a woman dressed in black. Nobody has ever managed to identify this elusive pair.

Albury

East of Clandon House stands the venue for easily the most famous, but most elusive ghost in Surrey: Emma the Saxon Maiden. According to the best-known version of this tale, the phantom is that of a beautiful local girl who lived with her father, a woodcutter, and mother in a cottage that stood not far from the Silent Pool east of Albury. This Emma was in the habit of bathing in the Silent Pool on warm summer's evenings.

Clandon Park is an eighteenth-century mansion built in the Palladian style by the Italian architect Giacomo Leoni to be the home of the great Oslow family. The grounds are haunted by the phantom of a nineteenth-century member of the family.

The Silent Pool sits at the foot of the North Downs and is
a famously tranquil spot. The equally famous phantom has
proved to be remarkably difficult to identify with any certainty.

The infamous ghostly coach of Abinger careers up the hill before stopping in the road between the Abinger Hatch pub and the church opposite. There it waits, as if for a passenger, before galloping off again. The origins of the haunting are obscure.

One such evening she was swimming naked in the pure waters when she heard the sounds of horses' hooves approaching. Appearing on the shores of the small lake came a group of richly clad noblemen, accompanied by tough soldiers. Unknown to poor Emma, one of the men was the wicked King John – treacherous brother to Good King Richard the Lionheart. Sighting the bashful peasant girl, the prince and his cronies snatched up her clothes and began shouting out ribald jests and lewd suggestions. Fearing for her safety and her honour, Emma waded further and further out into the small lake. Suddenly she missed her footing and fell headlong into the lake. There she drowned.

When Emma's father came looking for his daughter he found her sad body floating in the Silent Pool, while the hoof prints along the shore told their own story. He also found a cap caught in a tree and took this clue to his local vicar. The vicar in turn contacted Stephen Langton, Archbishop of Canterbury and a Surrey man born and bred. It did not take much detective work for Langton to discover that King John had lost just such a cap. Langton confronted John with the evidence and demanded that the king should pay compensation to the aggrieved father of Emma and do penance for his sins. John just laughed. It was this incident that convinced the barons that they could not expect to get justice from John. This in turn spurred them to seek to establish that even the king is not above the law, a campaign that did not end until the issuing of the Magna Carta at Runneymede in 1215.

Still unquiet, the ghost of Emma the beautiful Saxon maiden continues to haunt the Silent Pool. She appears naked, splashing and gambolling among the waters.

It is a great story, but unfortunately it is not true. Magna Carta was, indeed, forced upon King John by nobles led by Langton who wanted to ensure that the king had to obey the law, but their grievances had nothing to do with a Saxon girl from Albury. The entire story was concocted by a local antiquarian named Martin Tupper in the mid-nineteenth century. At least, almost all of it was. There had long been a tradition that the Silent Pool was haunted by a beautiful young woman swimming naked in the waters. It seems that Tupper grafted his romantic tale on to a pre-existing legend. Sadly, the fictional tale has replaced whatever was known about the ghost and her true identity remains unknown.

Abinger

Another enigmatic ghost is the ghost coach of Abinger. This dramatic phantom takes the form of an open carriage pulled by two horses. The vehicle comes galloping down Abinger Lane, sweeps past the Abinger Hatch and the ancient St James's Church, careering down the hill towards the Tilling Bourne stream. Opinion among those I talked to about this ghost was divided between those who thought it was linked to the pub and those who thought it had something to do with the church. One person told me that the pub used to attract passing coach trade – though this village is off the old coaching routes – and that the ghost is that of one such passer-by. Another was of the opinion that the coach called to collect the soul of 'some rich bloke from way back who is buried in the churchyard'. You can, I suppose, take your choice.

The church here, incidentally, was almost utterly destroyed on 18 August 1944 when it was hit by a V1 flying bomb, or doodle-bug, launched by the Germans as part of a salvo of thousands of such weapons thrown at southern England. An official report summed up the damage:

> The west wall of the nave, including the belfry and spire and the great tie beam on which they were supported, plus all the roof of the nave, were completely demolished. So too was the south door and porch, a great part of the north wall, including three Norman windows, and the south wall up to a point beyond the porch. The blast stripped all the roofs of the building, and the lych-gate, of their traditional Horsham stone slabs except for parts of the north face of the north aisle. Fragments of glass from all the windows lay outside.

The pub was also damaged, having its windows blown in and much of its roof stripped off.

Abinger Church, outside which the Abinger coach halts, is not all it seems. Of Norman origin, the church was almost totally destroyed by a V1 flying bomb in 1944 and has been rebuilt.

Friday Street

Just to the east lies Friday Street with its famous great pond and pub. The pub is named the Stephen Langton and although it looks ancient was in fact built only in 1930. It is named after a local lad who was born here in 1150. Young Stephen Langton was a precociously bright boy who had his education paid for by the local lord of the manor. He went on to study at the University of Paris, entered the Church and in 1207 was elected Archbishop of Canterbury. Not bad for a boy from a sleepy Surrey hamlet.

The phantom here, however, is almost certainly very much older than either the pub or the man it is named for. It is said that the pond is haunted by a beautiful young woman of vengeful nature. She appears in a most seductive guise and seeks to lure young men into the pond, where she pounces on them and forces them under the surface to drown. According to some versions of the story the phantoms of her victims also haunt this quiet spot.

When I visited the pub in 2010 I could not find anyone who had seen any such ghosts. The barman declared the story was nonsense. A possible clue to what might be going on here lies in the name of the little village. It is named for a pagan goddess of the English: Frijj or Freya. This goddess was a beautiful young woman who presided over love and marriage, but also had a more earthy sexual role. In one famous story she

The lake at Friday Street, which is
said to be haunted by a seductive
but deadly female phantom.

The village of Friday Street takes its name from
the pagan English goddess Frijj, a goddess of
fertility and rejoicing, about whom relatively little
is known. It has been speculated that the 'ghost'
of Friday Street is, in fact, Frige.

agreed to sleep with a hero in return for some fabulous jewellery. Using seductive beauty to lure young men to their deaths seems to be the sort of behaviour that the goddess Frijj might have enjoyed. Perhaps we have an ancient myth masquerading as a modern ghost.

South Holmwood

Definitely more modern, but no less enigmatic, is the ghost said to haunt the A24 at South Holmwood. Between Mill Road and Folly Lane the main road is now a dual carriageway and it would appear that the works involved in turning the old single carriageway road into a modern highway has frightened off the ghost, or rather ghosts. Back in the days before the roadworks there was a pub called the Holly and Laurel on the west side of the road. It is an inn no longer; the building is now a shop called The Emporium.

What is now the A24 was once a main coaching route and the phantoms date back to that time. Apparently a rider – he may have been a messenger – was galloping from London south to Horsham and on to Worthing. As he came to the Holly and Laurel his horse shied, reared and threw him badly. The man was terribly injured and was carried into the pub while a doctor was summoned. As he lay in agony the man gasped out that his horse had been frightened by a tall black man, who had mysteriously vanished. The doctor soon arrived, but it did the injured man no good and he died soon afterwards. The ghost of the rider was seen several times after this bizarre accident recreating the accident that cost him his life. Of the phantom black man nothing was ever seen again. For some reason the good folk of South Holmwood became convinced that the figure had been that of a ghostly Australian Aborigine – though why they should have thought so is obscure.

Dorking

North up the A24 lies the town of Dorking. The main road now bypasses the town centre, of course, so travellers need to turn off the A24 to get into the town centre. The roundabout where you need to turn west is dominated by a gigantic stainless steel chicken, so it is hard to miss. The chicken refers to the Dorking Hen, a breed of domestic fowl that is black and white in plumage and a famously good layer.

The road from the giant chicken leads into the High Street, on which stands the most famous haunted building in Dorking:

The door to the haunted Room 16 at the White Horse Hotel in Dorking. The lady phantom is perfectly friendly and does little to disturb guests.

The top floor of the Surrey Hills antiques shop in Dorking where a ghostly lady is said to walk. Interestingly those who see her invariably call her a lady, never a mere woman.

The White Horse Hotel. Tales and stories about this ancient inn abound. In origin it was a local commandery for the Knights Templar, that mysterious brotherhood of religious knights. The Templars were dedicated to protecting pilgrims in the Holy Land and maintained a sizeable private army to fight the Muslim Saracens. They paid for their military activities by renting out lands that had been donated to them across Christian Europe. The commanderies were local bases where Templars could stay when on their travels and where they collected rents, recruited soldiers and organised their business. The Templars have featured heavily in the books by Dan Brown and the White Horse has gained custom from those eager to stay in an old Templar building. It is rumoured that the Templars carried out secretive rituals in the cellars and one room is said to have been the site of a beheading.

In fact it is only the cellars and foundations that date back to Templar days; most of the above ground structure was erected on the old foundations in the 1740s, when it was rebuilt as a state-of-the-art coaching inn. Apart from a new wing at the back, the structure has not changed much since then. Dickens stayed here and it features in some of his works.

The main bar is said to be haunted by Charles Howard, who was also Earl of Surrey – though he is known to history by the title he inherited later in life, the 11th Duke of Norfolk. Born in 1746, Howard inherited the Surrey title from his father in 1777. He married in 1771, but his wife unfortunately went mad some ten years later. Surrey arranged for her care, renounced his Catholic faith and embarked on a political career. In London he met and fell in love with Mary Gibbon, sister of the famous historian Edward Gibbon. Unable to divorce his wife, Howard set up home with Mary not far from Dorking at Deepdene House. When travelling back and forth to London, Howard would catch the coach from the White Horse and was a familiar figure in the bar while waiting for the coach. Presumably he liked it so much he has never wanted to leave.

Quite unrelated to Howard is the ghost that lurks in Room 16. The ghost here is of a lady in a cloak who stands by the foot of the huge four-poster bed that dominates the room. She appears most often to guests, but staff have seen her as well. When I called, the manager, James Smith, was happy to talk about this ghost. 'There was one time in the bathroom when several tiles flew off the wall right out of the blue. The maid who witnessed the event said it was as if a heavy blow had been struck on the wall from behind, but the room it backs on to was empty at the time. It can be quite frightening for staff.'

At the western end of the High Street lies the aptly named West Street where No.17 is occupied by an antiques shop, though the property used to be a funeral parlour. The ghost here is of a lady, but although she has been seen by staff regularly little is known of her. A couple of doors away stands Christique Antiques. This property is haunted by a gentleman dating back to Tudor times who is known as 'Ben'. Whether this is his real name or not, Ben seems to prefer the downstairs rooms. Here he is seen most often beside the fireplace, standing apparently deep in thought. Ben is described as wearing a dark coat or cloak, with a white ruff around the neck. His face is

rarely seen as he is usually seen from behind. One person who used to work here told me that she enjoyed Ben's appearances. 'He was always such a comforting chap,' she said.

Almost opposite Christiques stands a shop called Surrey Hills, which occupies a 300-year-old town house. The first floor is home to a lady dressed in grey who potters about on mysterious business of her own. A former owner, Gloria Embury, reported:

> Once I was in there and we were sitting downstairs waiting to close up because we thought there was a customer upstairs. We waited for a while and then realised that there was nobody there at all. My staff were always seeing the lady.

Also in West Street stands an ancient house that was once home to one William Mullins. Now almost forgotten in his home town, Mullins was one of the passengers on the ship *Mayflower* which set sail in 1620 to found what was to become Massachusetts and the basis of British power in North America, and then of the United States of America. Mullins took with him his seventeen-year-old daughter Priscilla, who lived the rest of her life in America. She survived famine and disease until 1680 and had

Priscilla Mullins once lived in West Street, Dorking, but in 1620 she emigrated to North America to join one of the fledgling colonies. She married in America, riding to church in a most unusual procession. The ghost of her father haunts their old home.

THE BRIDAL PROCESSION

ten children by her husband, John Alden. Among her descendents was to be the nineteenth-century American poet Henry Wadsworth Longfellow. Mullins also had an older son and daughter, but they opted to stay in Dorking where they lived prosperous but unremarkable lives.

A figure in a dark suit and breeches that haunts this house is usually identified as being the ghost of William Mullins. The phantom comes up the stairs from the cellar, turns towards the front door and then vanishes.

Polesden Lacey

To the west of Dorking stands the lovely old house of Polesden Lacey, a beautiful Regency house on the site of a medieval manor house that was once home to the playwright Richard Brinsley Sheridan. It is appropriate, therefore, that the house boasts an outside theatre where events are held in the summer months. In the vast 1,400 acre grounds is a long path known as the Nun's Walk. It might be expected that a ghostly nun prowls here, but the ghost is in fact that of a rather shapeless, swirling mass of grey mist that races along the path. Elsewhere there is an ornamental bridge which is haunted by a sad figure in a brown cloak who exudes a feeling of melancholy.

At the far southern edge of the Polesden Lacey estate lies Ranmore Common. Close to the junction of Ranmore Road and Ranmore Common Road stands the Church of St Barnabas. This magnificent Victorian structure with its imposing spire was erected in 1860 and has been adopted as the church of the North Downs Way. The path between the church and road junction is the haunt of a figure dressed in tweeds. This chap is said to be fairly elderly, but I have not been able to find out much more about him.

Wotton

South again lies the little village of Wotton, best known for Wotton House. It was here that the diarist John Evelyn was born in 1620. The house was home to the Evelyns from its construction in the sixteenth century until the twentieth century, when it was sold. Since then it has served as a training college for firemen, a school and now a hotel and conference centre complete with indoor swimming pool, sauna and steam room and fitness centre. The sightings of the ghost here come mostly from the days when it was in the hands of the fire service.

The clearest view of the ghost was had by Mr Welch, a night porter who worked here in the 1960s. On 2 April 1964 he was on duty as usual when, just before 3 a.m., he took a rest at the reception desk before resuming his patrols. He heard the front door open and close, which came as a surprise since the door was locked shut. Then a man dressed in 'a hairy brown tweed jacket and dark trousers' walked into the hallway. Tucked under his arm the figure carried what Welch took to be a fishing rod, though he could not be sure. The figure strolled across the hall, and then halted. Thinking the figure was a real human, Welch asked if he could help at all. The man had a calm face and peaceful bearing. He ignored Welch's question and continued across the hall towards a door. Just as he approached the door, the figure vanished into thin air – which was when Welch realised that he had seen a ghost. Other night staff reported hearing footsteps and seeing a vague figure in the hall, but none saw the ghost as well as Welch did.

The elegant spire of the Church of St Barnabus at Ranmore soars high into the sky on the summit of the North Downs. The old boy dressed in tweeds who haunts the path beside the church is seen fairly often.

The Guildford Road at Great Bookham is said to be haunted by a ghostly coach, about which nothing certain is known.

The large panelled room on the first floor used for lectures and talks was also said to be haunted. Several staff reported hearing footsteps here, and others complained of a sudden and supernaturally deep drop in temperature. One at least refused to enter the room, saying that it was 'evil'.

On 19 July 1893 the then owner of Wotton House, William Evelyn, was eating lunch in the dining room with his brother and two friends. They were interrupted by a figure waving at them from the window that looked over the terrace. Evelyn and his brother both recognised it as the old family friend, Samuel Wilberforce, the Bishop of Winchester. Wilbeforce was waving in agitated fashion as if wanting Evelyn to go outside to meet him. Evelyn was surprised that his old friend would arrive without

giving advance notice, and even more so that he had not called at the front door, but he slipped out nonetheless. There was no sign of Wilberforce on the terrace and subsequent searches by the four men failed to find the aged bishop. In fact, Wilberforce was at that very moment lying dead in Deerlap Wood at Holmbury St Mary, having been thrown by his horse.

Great Bookham

North from the little cluster of haunted sites in and around Dorking is Great Bookham. The Guildford Road here is said to be haunted by a ghostly coach. Some say that only the sounds of the passing horses and wheels can be heard and that nothing is seen. Give the heavy traffic on this road, it would be remarkable if anything is heard at all.

Leatherhead

East of Great Bookham stands Leatherhead, an old market town that seems to derive its name from a pre-Roman term translating as 'The Grey Ford'. The town was modernised in the 1980s to include a pedestrianised town centre, bypass road and extensive car parking. Remaining from the old days is the town's parish church of St Mary and St Nicholas in Church Road. The church began as an abbey founded by King Edward the Confessor in the 1050s, but at the Reformation the abbey was closed and the church became the parish church. A few fragments of wall remain from Edward's day, but most of what stands today is fourteenth century in date. In the fifteenth century a tower was added that stands at an odd angle to the nave.

The haunting of the church and its grounds must be ancient, as it is the ghost of a monk who walks here. Written accounts date back only to the 1950s, however, and no trace of a phantom before that date can be found. The ghostly monk wears a typical monkish robe and hood. He walks slowly, and vanishes within a second or two of being seen.

Merry Hall is perhaps the finest house in Ashtead, although its once extensive grounds have been reduced by housing developments. The ghosts here take the unusual form of thoroughbred racehorses.

A ghost that is no longer seen was once very active around the junction of High Street and Bridge Street. This is now part of the pedestrianised area, which may be why the ghost is no longer seen. In 1930 a woman was knocked down and killed here on a foggy night by a motorist who was not driving as slowly as he should have been. Late at night the ghost of the unfortunate victim would appear, stepping out straight in front of approaching vehicles. When the motorist slammed on his brakes, convinced that he had hit the woman, there was nobody to be seen. The police reportedly got fed up with being called to non-existent accidents. The ghost has not been seen since cars ceased using this road.

Across the M25 to the east lies Ashtead – once a tiny hamlet but since the railway came in Victorian times a bustling commuter suburb. A rare survivor from the pre-railway days is Merry Hall in Agates Lane, a fine Georgian mansion. For many years in the mid-twentieth century this was home to the writer John Beverley Nichols, who produced a string of novels, most of which featured gardens and gardening. Back in the 1880s Merry Hall was home to a racehorse owner by the name of J.C. Masterman. In 1890 his horse, Ilex, won the Grand National. Three years later Masterman fell seriously ill and the doctors soon realised that he was dying. The family arranged for his beloved racehorses to be brought to Merry Hall to be paraded around the grounds so that the ailing Masterman could see them for one last time. Ilex was among them. Since then the ghostly parade of horses has been seen, as has a sad-faced man in riding clothes who is taken to be one of the grooms.

Epsom

North-east of Ashtead is Epsom, once a spa town but now rather more famous for its horseracing. Between the town centre and the racecourse there once stood the grand house of Pitt Place, home to Lord Lyttleton. Lyttleton was an infamous rake who had set up home with three sisters aged fifteen, seventeen and nineteen – the Amphlett girls from Worcestershire. It was not entirely clear if Lyttleton had seduced only the eldest sister, Margaret, or all three. What was known was that the girls' mother, the widowed Mrs Amphlett, had died of a broken heart soon after the girls had moved in with Lyttleton.

On the evening of 25 November 1779 Lyttleton was upstairs at Pitt Place when he saw the ghost of Mrs Amphlett appear in front of him. 'You will join me in three days,' declared the apparition, before vanishing. Lyttleton laughed off the threat and spent the next three days partying around Epsom - including an event at the Assembly Rooms, now a pub, in the High Street. But three days later to the hour he collapsed and by the time a doctor arrived he was dead.

Ewell

North from Epsom is Ewell, a pretty little village built around the headwaters of the Hogsmill River that is now bypassed by the A140 dual carriageway. The High Street here is haunted by a ghostly coach and four - or at least, it was. I have failed to find anyone who has seen this apparition in recent years.

Rather more active are the ghostly children of St Mary's, off the London Road. In 1665 the dreaded plague arrived in Ewell from London. In this little village the

The modern Bourne Hall was built on the site of the old mansion that once stood in the heart of Ewell. The ghosts that wander the grounds date back to the time of the original house.

The Victorian artist Holman Hunt was confronted by an unnerving phantom in Ewell High Street one night and was left shaking with fear.

horrific disease proved to be especially fatal to children and almost an entire generation of youngsters fell victim in less than a month. The pitiful bodies were buried in a corner of the churchyard. The ghosts of these youngsters have been seen around the church ever since.

In the middle of the town is Bourne Hall, a modernist library and leisure complex built on the site of the original manor house. The grounds are open to the public and provide pleasant paths to stroll, ducks for children to feed and a string of ornamental ponds and streams. The grounds are the haunt of a lady in eighteenth-century dress who walks quietly about her own business. One witness told me that she remained in sight for quite a long time, but vanished as soon as he started to walk towards her.

Ewell was the home for the great pre-Raphaelite artist Holman Hunt, who would commute to London by train. One winter's evening he was walking home from Ewell West station – remember this was before the days of street lighting – when he found himself confronted by a tall white figure which blocked his path. The figure lunged forward and promptly vanished into thin air, leaving a very startled artist.

Nonsuch Park

East of Ewell is the vast Nonsuch Park, once the site of a palace built by Henry VIII. The palace was demolished in 1682, but the deer park remained and is now owned by the local council. Near to the main south entrance the phantom figure of a tall man with a thin face, dark-coloured hat and long black overcoat has been seen. Local legend has it this is the ghost of a local Victorian gentleman who had

seduced the wife of a workman. He was in the habit of meeting his lover in the park before whisking her off for some illicit time together. The wronged husband found out about the affair and, according to one version told to me, donned his wife's cloak to go to meet the lover. Coming upon the man in the park, the husband pulled a knife and killed him on the spot. Another version sees the husband killing his wife and then himself, leaving the gentleman to blame himself for the deaths and pine away. Both versions cannot be true; perhaps neither is true. The ghost may be that of some perfectly harmless chap.

Tadworth Court

South of Ewell on the road to Reigate stands the beautiful early eighteenth-century Tadworth Court, venue for one of the best-known stories in Surrey. At some point in the eighteenth century, it is said, two sisters lived at Tadworth Court. When the elder sister turned eighteen her parents had her portrait painted and hung it over the staircase. The two teenage girls, meanwhile, had fallen in love with the same local man of good family. He preferred the elder sister, and the younger was driven to a jealous rage. The younger girl murdered the older, then committed suicide by hurling herself from the roof of the house.

A few days after the double funeral, the painting underwent a macabre change. Peering through a bush in the background could be made out a face. That face became clearer as the days passed and soon it was recognised as that of the younger sister, her features contorted with hate. The distraught family threw the picture out, but that prompted the ghost of the girls to stalk the house so it was brought back.

It has remained overlooking the staircase ever since, no matter how many times the house has changed ownership.

Although this story is widely known, it is sadly not true. No sisters died at Tadworth Court in suspicious circumstances, nor even close together. The story was invented to match the admittedly very odd picture of a pretty young woman with a hideous face peering at her from behind some bushes in the background.

Woodmansterne

Apparently much more real was the haunting of the house known as Fairlawns in Woodmansterne, a few miles north-east of Tadworth. The house has now gone, its place taken by a nest of residential roads off Croydon Lane. In 1948, however, the house became well known in the local press due to reports of three ghostly figures that were seen regularly walking through the grounds. The three were said to be two men and a woman dressed in what were described as medieval clothes. These sightings were followed by the sounds of footsteps in empty rooms within the house. The then owners held a séance, which failed totally to uncover any explanation for the hauntings. Although the séance was counted a failure at first, it was soon clear that the hauntings had ceased so it must have had some effect after all.

Purley

Further to the west still, the Royal Oak pub once stood in Brighton Road, Purley. The pub was a fairly modern structure, but this did not stop it being haunted by a genial old boy in a worn jacket and trousers. This was the ghost of a well-known local retired man who used to take his lunches regularly in the pub, and continued to return for some years after he died.

Riddlesdown

South-east of Purley are the steep-sided chalk hills of Riddlesdown. Riddlesdown Road is now not much more than a bridleway running along the top of the Riddles Down itself, but in years gone by this was the main road and what is now the A22 in the valley below was a mere path. At some point in the eighteenth century, nobody seems very clear when, a stagecoach running along the Riddlesdown Road overturned and tumbled down the steep escarpment – with fatal results for the driver. The ghostly coach is said to still travel the old road, its horses being lashed to a sweat by the phantom of the doomed driver.

A firm date for the coach crash at Warlingham does exist. In November 1809 a Royal Mail coach was heading north towards London along the Limpsfield Road, now the B269. As the coach came up the junction with Slines Oak Road, a highwayman stepped out with pistol drawn. The coach guard was not about to surrender easily and whipped out a blunderbuss. The exchange of gunfire that followed caused the coach horses to stampede, dragging the coach straight into Slines Pond, which lay nearby. According to legend, the coach returns in spectral form late at night to emerge dramatically from the pond with lanterns lit and passengers screaming in panic.

The junction of Abbots Lane and Hayes Lane in Kenley is haunted by an enigmatic phantom who may be linked to the village of Watendone, which stood here for centuries, but which was abandoned in the sixteenth century.

Coulsdon

To the west lies Hackbridge Road in Coulsdon. Although now heavily built up by twentieth-century housing estates, factories and offices, this was once a narrow rural lane. Back in 1803 a farmer was discovered dead in the road with his neck broken. There were rumours of murder, but the local coroner ruled the man had died due to a riding accident. It would seem that the rumours may have been true, for the farmer's ghost came back time and again. He was seen most recently in the 1950s outside the Red Lion pub.

To the east is Whyteleafe, connected to Kenley by Whyteleafe Hill Road. Until the 1930s this road was haunted by an old man carrying a lantern. The construction of houses along what had previously been a rural lane seems to have laid him to rest.

Kenley

Still very much about is the hooded figure seen lurking around the junction of Hayes Lane and Abbots Lane in Kenley. This figure is said by locals to be a nun, though there would not seem to be any evidence for this. One local variant of the story has it that the nun is looking for the lost chapel of Watendone. This was a village that was a thriving community at the time of the

Domesday Book in the eleventh century and which continued to be mentioned in various records over the next four centuries. It lay on the Downs west of Kenley and seems to have focussed on the wool trade.

By 1550 the village had vanished –either due to plague or economic decline. The chapel alone survived, served by the Kenley clergy on a very occasional basis. The chapel burned down in 1780 and the remaining walls were taken down so that the stones could be used elsewhere. The site was excavated in the 1960s. If the ghostly nun is looking for the chapel, she is unlikely to find it. Nothing now remains above ground.

Close to Kenley station, Hayes Lane crosses over the railway lines on a bridge. Loitering on this bridge, a man has been seen dressed in a suit of old-fashioned cut, some say from the 1930s. He seems to be lost in thought, staring down at the railway lines as if for inspiration. He vanishes if approached. South of the station, the Godstone Road is said to be haunted by a coach and four, but I can find scant evidence for this.

Bletchingley

Further south still on the southern edge of the Downs is the village of Bletchingley, astride the A25. In medieval times this was an important market borough, but after about 1450 it lost trade to Reigate and slipped into quiet village status. Except

Bletchingley church is haunted by a lady in seventeenth-century garb. She has been tentatively identified as being a Mrs Clayton, who is buried here.

at election times, that is, for Bletchingley retained its two MPs until the Great Reform Act of 1832.

The oldest building in the village is the Church of St Mary the Virgin, the tower of which was built in 1090 and most of the rest some three centuries later. The south aisle is dominated by the great tomb of Robert Clayton and his wife. Born into relatively humble circumstances in 1629, Clayton was apprenticed to a scrivener in the City of London. He later set up his own business, amassing so much wealth that he was able to found his own bank, which in turn made him even richer. He commissioned this tomb in 1704, and died three years later. The ghostly lady of Bletchingley is seen most often near this tomb, though she has been seen in other parts of the church and churchyard. Her clothing would seem to date her to the late seventeenth century, so perhaps she is Clayton's wife (who died a few years before him and was buried in the same tomb).

Another ghostly lady haunts the Red Lion in Castle Street. This lovely old building has parts dating back to 1309, though it was heavily remodelled in the eighteenth century and has recently undergone a refurbishment. Before the recent changes to make this into a superb dining pub, the lady in grey was a regular visitor. She stalked the corridors and the narrow passageway on the first floor. Her footsteps were heard more often than she was seen herself, but she was a regular presence.

Limpsfield

Rather larger than Bletchingley is Limpsfield, a few miles to the east along the A25. The northern end of the High Street around the church is haunted by a grey lady. She is said by locals to be the ghost of a young woman who lived at New Hall, but she moved her haunting ground to the High Street after that building was demolished. Even more elusive is the phantom of St Andrews Way, which, strictly speaking, stands in Limpsfield Chart, a hamlet just south of Limpsfield. The street is reportedly haunted by a grey figure, accompanied by a whooshing sound.

Oxted

Adjacent to Limpsfield is Oxted. Standing at 53 High Street is the Crown Inn, which can boast of two ghosts. The more active of the two is a lady who stalks the upstairs area late at night. She is said to be a former landlady. Those who have seen her seem undecided as to whether she is wearing a nightdress or a long white gown. Given that she is seen only after dark, a nightdress might seem more suitable. One witness said that moments before the ghostly lady appeared the temperature in the room dropped suddenly and dramatically. It was so cold that he could see his breath condensing in front of him, even though it was a warm June evening. The second ghost manifests itself in the bar, usually by the fireplace. He is not seen so often as the lady upstairs and appears to be unconnected to her. At any rate, there are no stories attached to him.

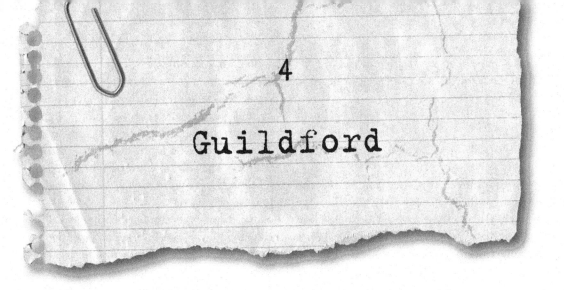

4

Guildford

THE county town of Guildford takes its name from the golden sand beside the ford that made this an ideal place to cross the River Wey. The sand is still there, albeit mostly buried under buildings, but the ford has long since been replaced by a succession of bridges. The town did not exist in Roman times, but was a thriving English town by about AD 600 and has remained a busy market town ever since. William the Conqueror built a castle to dominate the town, and the main keep and some walls of the fortress still stand. The modern growth of the town began in 1653 when the Wey was dredged out from the Thames to Guildford, making the town an inland port that handled goods heading south into the Weald. Today the town has a human population of about 68,000, and its supernatural population is equally impressive.

AA Headquarters

For many years the most famous haunted building in Guildford was the AA Headquarters, officially Fanum House, on the roundabout where the London Road met the Ladymead Parkway, a twentieth-century bypass around the town centre. The office building was a fine brick edifice with a distinctive clock tower. As a boy, I was frequently driven past it with the family on our way into Guildford and years later I travelled past it daily on my way to work. I recall often hearing about the ghost there when I was younger.

I was told that the phantom in question was that of a cleaning lady who had died sometime in the 1950s. She came back after office hours, as she had done when alive, to potter about the building. It was presumed by the night staff who encountered her that she was intent on cleaning. The most frequent manifestation was the flushing of toilets, the turning on or off of taps and other plumbing-related activity. There were also the sounds of ashtrays being emptied, bins banged about and broom sweeping on the hard floors. Just occasionally the cleaner's voice would be heard, coming from empty rooms or echoing along empty corridors. She was also seen sometimes, walking slowly dressed in a purple, wrap-around cleaning overall of the type worn by 'Mrs Mops' back in the 1950s and 1960s. A few years ago the old Fanum House was demolished and a new one built. The ghost may have been very active in the old AA HQ, but she has not been seen or heard in the new one.

The Old Chalk Pit

AA members may no longer see the ghost at their HQ, but they may find one if they drive their cars along York Road that branches off London Road, half a mile towards the town centre from the AA roundabout. Until the 1960s there was an old chalk pit in York Road that had an evil reputation locally. It was said to be haunted and was certainly the venue for ne'erdowells to gather of an evening.

In 1969 a multi-storey car park was built in the chalk pit, and that was when the haunting first hit the local news headlines. Workmen reported seeing a woman dressed in a long dress, variously described as being grey or pale brown in colour. She was seen amid the construction equipment, but could never be found when a search was made. The workmen declared her to be a ghost and became uneasy about working alone or after dark.

An old story then surfaced about a local girl named Lorna Smith. She had been the daughter of a Quaker merchant who lived in Guildford in the later eighteenth century. Lorna's father found her late one evening consorting with a good-looking local lad who was not only poor but – rather more seriously for the angry father – was a Catholic. Lorna had been dragged home by her father to be subjected to a torrent of

The shop at No. 122 High Street, Guildford, is rumoured to have a ghost on the first floor, but witnesses appear to be difficult to find.

angry abuse. The distraught girl fled in the night, heading for the home of her beloved, but in the dark she fell into the chalk pit and broke her neck. Perhaps the unhappy Lorna was disturbed by all the work going on in the old chalk pit, and she came back to see what was happening.

No. 122 High Street

In the town centre the ancient, cobbled High Street runs down a fairly steep hill from what was once the bailey of the castle to the bridge that now takes the place of the ford. One of the shops is a ladies' fashion store at No. 122. In here is one of those irritating hauntings that a lot of people have heard about, but which nobody seems to have experienced first hand. There is said to be a lady who walks across the first floor. Her heels are heard quite clearly, but she herself remains invisible.

Angel Hotel

A few steps down the hill from No.122 and on the other side of the road is the old Angel Hotel. This building opened to the public in the late sixteenth century as a posting house, a place where the coaches carrying urgent messages between London and the naval base and port of Portsmouth would change their horses while drivers and passengers grabbed something to eat and drink. The site, and some of the original buildings, had been the guest house of the Whitefriars Monastery that stood in Guildford, and parts of the structure date back to about 1250. The building has been changed many times over the years, but it remains a fine historic inn.

Perhaps the most haunted street in Surrey is the High Street in Guildford, where several shops and pubs have ghostly tales attached to them.

In the 1870s the hotel was temporary home to the dashing young Louis Napoleon, Prince Imperial of France. His father, Emperor Napoleon III, had been ousted from his throne after losing the Franco-Prussian War of 1870 and the family came to Britain. The young prince joined the British Royal Artillery and was deemed to be a most promising young officer. Although he was the last male heir of the Bonaparte dynasty, he insisted on being treated like any other young officer so that he could earn a military reputation to follow that of his family. He stayed at the Angel when entertaining guests coming to visit him on manoeuvres at nearby Aldershot Camp. In 1879 the Prince Imperial joined the British Army invading Zulu land in southern Africa. His patrol was ambushed by Zulus and the young man died bravely, fighting on with a spear taken from a dead Zulu after his ammunition gave out.

Until 2001 the grand door to No. 132 High Street, Guildford, gave access to a gunsmith's, but it has now vanished. The haunting here is that of the firm's founder, Jack Jeffrey, but he has not been seen since his business left.

The stories of a haunting at the Angel began soon afterwards. The ghost of a young man in military uniform was reported in Rooms 1 and 2, those used most often by the Prince Imperial. The clearest sighting came in 1970 when a Mr and Mrs Dell were staying in Room 1. Something woke Mr Dell up early and as he glanced about the room he saw a man in a uniform standing beside a heavy wardrobe. The man had a thick, black moustache, heavy eyebrows and eyes that seemed to be sad or melancholy. Mr Dell sat looking at the man for sometime, then woke up his wife who saw the apparition briefly before it vanished.

Mr Dell subsequently found some pictures of the Prince Imperial, but decided that the ghost did not resemble the young man. The ghost had looked to be about forty-five or so, while the prince had been only twenty-three when he was killed. However, the uniform did seem to be that of a late nineteenth-century cavalry officer. Perhaps the ghost was that of an aide or a colleague of the unfortunate prince.

No. 132 High Street

At No. 132 High Street is another ladies' fashion shop, but from 1863 to 2001 it was home to the famous Jeffrey's Gunsmiths business. In 1928 the shop was inherited by two brothers, Jack and Harold, who ran the business jointly. As the brothers grew older they hired a manager, Mr Hall, to run the shop for them, though they still came in to keep an eye on things. A small office down in the basement was set aside for the two Mr Jeffreys. In 1970 Harold died, and Jack followed him in 1979. Mr Hall stayed on to run the business for the new owners.

It was just after Jack Jeffrey's funeral that the haunting began, and it was the office

Tudor Lounge Restaurant

The Tudor Lounge Restaurant at No. 144 High Street has a ghost that is most certainly active. Nobody knows whose ghost this is, but she has been seen clearly by several witnesses. She is a lady of about sixty years of age who is said to be quite short, perhaps about 5ft 2ins or so. She is seen most often close to the window on the first floor. People both inside the restaurant and outside have seen the spectral figure staring out of the window as if scanning the High Street for someone. Perhaps she is waiting for somebody who never arrived when she was alive.

Three other spectral women in the High Street are rather less benign. These three unfortunates were hanged for witchcraft-related crimes in the 1650s. Contrary to popular belief, English law had never imposed the death penalty for witchcraft, only for crimes such as murder, theft or wounding carried out by means of witchcraft. No doubt it was a fine distinction beyond the interest of the three witches of Guildford as they were led to the scaffold. The local people clearly believed these particular women to be guilty of witchcraft. They may indeed have been guilty of causing injury to their neighbours. In pre-modern rural communities there was much need for a local person who understood the medicinal properties of herbs and plants. Such wise women could, if unscrupulous enough, use their knowledge to poison livestock, claiming that they were using magical powers, and so extort money from their neighbours. Whatever the truth, the three women were hanged and their souls

in the cellar that was the focus for events. Old Jack Jeffrey was seen several times in the small office, sitting as if going through the accounts or reading a newspaper. So far as I can tell he was never seen in the public parts of the shop, but the staff were more than familiar with his appearances. After Jeffrey's vacated the shop, it was remodelled and the cellar cleared of all internal partitions, including that of the small office. Opinions differ as to whether the ghost has been seen since.

The poltergeist of the Three Pigeons pub in Guildford is unique in paranormal annals since it manifested itself in three separate visitations, in 1976, 1988 and 2003. As a rule, poltergeists take up residence in a building only once, though they may stay for some months before departing.

The ghost of the Royal Grammar School in Guildford may not be all that it seems, though a real event may lie behind the story.

have prowled the High Street ever since. It is said that they take the form of black shadows in ill-lit corners at night, waiting to pounce out on unwary passers-by.

Three Pigeons Public House

At No. 169 High Street stands thee Three Pigeons pub, a historic building dating back to the 1720s. In 1976 the pub was taken as a residence by a poltergeist. The initial visitation lasted for about a year, then faded away – only to return in 1988. After some more months of activity, the poltergeist left again, but came back in 2003. At the time of writing it is quiet again, but who knows when it may return. Fortunately this particular pol-

tergeist seems to be more mischievous than dangerous. It delights in switching lights on and off, disconnecting pipes from beer taps, slamming doors or moving furniture about.

Royal Grammar School

Near the top of the High Street stands the Royal Grammar School. Founded in 1510, the school has been educating local boys to a high standard for five centuries and occupies a range of buildings that date from every century of its existence. Among the school's claims to fame is the fact that the oldest recorded game of cricket (called 'krekett' in the document) was played by its boys. The ghost is said to be that of an old boy who was killed when out hunting somewhere nearby. His ghost is supposed to ride up to the gates of the school mounted on a terrifyingly lively grey stallion. The rider throws open the gates, approaches the building known as Big School, and rides through the doors and up the stairs, where he vanishes.

Although the ghost is fairly well known, it would seem that this is an example of a local event getting muddled up and turned into a ghost story. Back in the 1920s an ex-pupil really did ride his horse into the school and up the stairs – but there was nothing supernatural about it. He did it for a bet.

Abbot's Hospital

Our final ghost in Guildford's much haunted High Street is to be found at the Abbot's Hospital, or more properly the Hospital of the Blessed Trinity. Built by George Abbot in 1619 to house poor single elderly folk, the Hospital has been extended and renovated over the years so that it can now house twenty-six locals of good standing.

On 12 July 1685 a column of soldiers came into Guildford from the west, dragging with them a prisoner. The man in chains was the Duke of Monmouth, on his way to trial for High Treason in London. When King Charles II died in 1685 the crown passed to his unpopular Catholic brother James II. Monmouth, however, was not only popular but he was a Protestant and, for good measure, was a son of Charles II. Monmouth had been born when Charles II was living in exile after the English Civil War and everyone had assumed that his mother, Lucy Walters, had been one of Charles's numerous mistresses and girlfriends. However, Monmouth then produced documents that showed that his parents had gone through a marriage ritual – though the legality of the marriage was seriously in doubt – and claimed the throne for himself. He raised a small army and invaded England. He was defeated at the Battle of Sedgemoor, captured and by the time he reached Guildford was on his way to London for inevitable execution. Monmouth had already appealed to his uncle for mercy, but King James had curtly dismissed the plea.

Monmouth was put on trial, found guilty and on 15 July taken to the scaffold. James acted with great harshness towards those who had supported Monmouth, ordering hundreds of executions and sending to the scaffold even those who had been only marginally involved. The harshness caused James to become even more unpopular than he had already been and three years later he was ousted in a coup organised by a group of nobles and army officers. Monmouth, meanwhile, was dead. The figure seen lurking in the room in the gatehouse where Monmouth had been imprisoned is usually identified as being the ghost of Monmouth.

When I spoke to the current occupant of the Tower Room in the spring of 2010, he told me that he has never been disturbed by the ghost, though he is an admittedly heavy sleeper. All the tales of the ghost – and some of them are very vivid – date back more than fifty years. Perhaps this is another of those phantoms that has run out of energy and ceased appearing.

A second ghostly manifestation has been reported here. Late at night the sounds of jollity and partying have been heard coming from a first-floor room overlooking the courtyard. The noises are heard only when the room is empty, and no explanation for them has been found.

It is a sad phantom who is said to haunt the Abbot's Hospital in Guildford. The Duke of Monmouth came to England in 1685 hoping to become king, but ended up on the scaffold.

Loseley Park is said to be home to several ghosts, but the More-Molyneux family who live here treat them as part of the family and prefer not to talk about them. (Courtesy of Andrew Wilkinson)

Shalford

Running south from the town is the Shalford Road, the A281, which runs through the little village of Shalford on its way to Horsham. In 1709 a miller lived here by the name of Christopher Slaughterford, who was engaged to a local farmer's daughter named Jane Young. One evening, after the pair had been out walking, Jane went missing. Slaughterford swore that he had waved her goodbye within sight of her home, but after her body was found bundled into a ditch he was arrested for murder.

There was no real evidence against Slaughterford, other than the fact that he was known to have been with the unfortunate woman on the night she died. However, he was not a popular man locally and the local jury seemed only too happy to put a sinister connotation on the flimsiest of evidence and Slaughterford was found guilty. He was hanged in Guildford on 9 July. A few months later a man working at the mill hanged himself. Investigations found that the man had himself been missing when Jane was murdered. Had he committed suicide out of remorse for seeing his employer hanged for a crime he himself had committed? Or was the suicide unrelated?

Whatever the truth of the tragedy, Slaughterford's ghost has been seen walking from the site of his execution in Guildford to his old home, the mill at Shalford. He is said to have a staff in one hand and a burning torch in the other. Given the huge volume of traffic on this road and the lack of reports recently, it would seem he walks no more.

Loseley House

A mile or two west of Shalford stands Loseley House. This fine mansion was built in the 1560s and is the seat of the More-Molyneux family. The house, which is open to the public, contains some splendid interior decorations and magnificent furniture. It is better known these days for the ice creams and yoghurts made from the milk provided by the estate's herd of jersey cows.

There are numerous stories about the hauntings of Loseley House. When I contacted the current Mr More-Molyneux he very politely informed me that 'we view our ghosts as members of the family and therefore do not divulge details on them'. That is fair enough, but it is perhaps worth recording what other locals have to say on the subject.

There are, it is said, three ghosts here. The 'Nice Lady' is the ghost of a Victorian housekeeper. She walks the house in a brown dress with a smile on her face, bringing in her wake an atmosphere of calm and serenity. The 'Nasty Lady' is altogether different. She stomps about, scowling, and exudes a feeling of anger, hatred and hostility. It is said that she was the lady of the manor in the seventeenth century. For reasons long forgotten, she killed her own son in a fit of temper by hurling him into the moat that then surrounded the house. She was swiftly overcome with remorse and lived the rest of her life in misery. The third ghost is that of the drowned child who is seen only rarely, flitting about the area of the gardens where the moat once stood.

Sutton Place

Just north-east of Guildford is Sutton Place, a Tudor manor house built in 1530 to replace a medieval manor mentioned in the Domesday Book. The house is private property, though its fine gatehouses stand on the A3 and are well-known landmarks. The ghost here is persistent and, apparently, very active. She is a lady dressed in white who is accompanied by the sounds of wooden furniture being smashed.

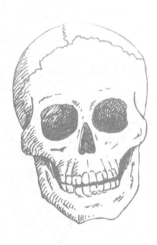

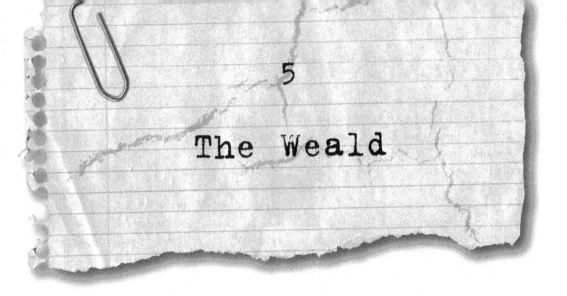

5

The Weald

STRETCHING across the southern half of Surrey, the Weald was for centuries a vast forest growing on wet, clay soils interspersed by a few villages and fewer roads. More modern farming techniques made the heavy soils more productive, and these days the dark forests have generally given way to open fields, while the villages and towns have grown greatly in size and prosperity. They have also grown a remarkable collection of ghosts to fascinate the visitor.

Lingfield

At the far eastern end of the Weald lies the village of Lingfield, now best known for the racecourse laid out on the banks of the Eden Brook. West of the village, Hare Lane runs out to Littlefield. This lane is haunted by a young couple, though it is the young woman who is seen more often than the young man. Those who have seen the phantom couple report that they stroll along quietly enough, most often at the upper or western end of the narrow lane.

In the village itself stands the ancient Greyhound Inn on Plaistow Street. The haunting here came to the notice of those outside the village in the 1970s, but it had been going on for a good few years by then. The majority of incidents occurred in the kitchens, though the skittle alley also saw some paranormal action. The incidents were rather vague, but nonetheless disquieting for those who experienced them. Small objects went missing, only to reappear again in full view. Members of staff felt a person touch them, only to find that they were alone. And there was the strong and irresistible feeling that somebody else was there - a feeling that would come and go.

In 1976 the then landlords, John and Audrey Chapman, sent for a local Caterham man named Eddie Pratt, who claimed to be a clairvoyant. Pratt would later have his gifts studied by a team at York University who reported that his abilities did seem to be out of the ordinary, though they could offer no explanation for them. Pratt visited the Greyhound and was shown around by John Chapman. As they entered the old skittle alley, the familiar feeling of somebody being present was felt by Chapman, who also reported a sudden chill in the air. Pratt also experienced the feeling and the chill. Looking around, he became aware of a boy

The young couple who haunt Hare Lane near Lingfield give every appearance of being blissfully happy and deeply in love. Who they might be is utterly obscure.

aged about eight years old who was apparently studying the two men intently. The boy was neatly dressed in a grey suit with rounded collars and a white shirt. The boy did not seem hostile, though nor was he entirely at ease. After a few seconds the boy faded away, and the chill went with him.

Looking for some identity for the phantom boy proved rather difficult. The Greyhound was built sometime before 1584, when it is first mentioned in written records, but its history is not well recorded. There was once a secret room off the skittle alley that could be accessed only through a sliding wooden panel. Tradition had it that this room was used by a gang of smugglers, who would stash rum and silks here on their way from the remoter coves on the Kent coast to the buying public in London.

It has had often been supposed that the phantom might have been linked in some way to this nefarious and dangerous trade. However, the heyday of such smugglers was in the mid- to late eighteenth century, while the ghostly boy's clothing placed him somewhere in the early nineteenth century.

Whoever the boy is, he seems to like the Greyhound and to enjoy his little pranks. He seems harmless enough and causes little real bother.

Puttenden Manor

On the Haxted Road, a mile or so north of Lingfield, stands Puttenden Manor (sometimes spelled Puttendon Manor). This lovely old house was built by a modestly wealthy landowner named Reginald Sondes in 1477. The Sondes family continued to prosper and by 1626 were doing so well that the heir to the lands, twenty-six-year-old George Sondes was created a knight during the traditional festivities that accompanied the coronation of King Charles I. Sondes proved to be loyal to his monarch and when Civil War came he and his family unhesitatingly backed the king against Parliament.

When Charles I was executed and Parliament ruled supreme it seemed as if Sondes had backed the wrong side. He was forced to pay a hefty fine and retired to his estates a considerably poorer man than he had been just a few years earlier. His younger son, Freeman, fell out with his father and his elder brother George over the turn of events – perhaps because the family no longer had enough money to set him up in his chosen career as a gentleman-mercenary. Such soldiers of fortune were a regular feature of life in Europe at the time. Young men of good family, sound education and adventurous spirit would join the army of some ruler or other to learn the trade of soldiering. If they survived they would generally be able to earn a good living as army officers. But first they had to pay for their own arms, clothes, supplies and horses during the years they spent gaining their experience.

In 1655 young Freeman returned to England in a foul temper. He met his elder brother at Lees Court, the family's main estate in Kent, and the two quarrelled violently. That night, as George lay sleeping, Freeman crept to his room armed with a dagger and a butcher's cleaver. The elder brother was murdered in brutal fashion. Freeman fled, but he did not get far. News of such a notorious murder spread quickly and Freeman was arrested as he tried to find a ship to carry him to France. On 25 August 1655 he was hanged on the gallows outside the town gates of Maidstone. The distraught Sir George and his wife Jane planted a pair of weeping willows overlooking the large pond in the grounds of his manor to remind him of his two lost sons. The double tragedy left Sondes' daughter, Lady Mary, as the heiress.

In 1660 King Charles II returned to regain his throne and the ever loyal Sir George saw his fortunes restored. He achieved high office and was created Earl of Faversham. Lady Mary married Louis de Duras, Marquis Blanquefort, a French nobleman who had come to England with King Charles II and who was highly regarded as both a soldier and a government administrator. The couple died childless, so the estates passed through various cousins to descend today to the current Countess Sondes. The ancestral manor is no longer inhabited by the family, who long ago moved to a grander residence near Faversham.

At least, it is not inhabited by any living members of the family. It is generally thought that the ghosts of Puttenden are those of Sir George and his wife, Lady Jane, who continue to walk the house and grounds mourning the tragic fate of their sons. The female ghost is seen more often, and heard even more frequently. She seems to prefer the upstairs rooms and one bedroom in particular. The sound of her dainty footsteps and swishing silk dress is heard quite often, usually accompanied by a distinctive scent of heavy perfume. When seen, she is wearing a long, full silk dress of the type fashionable in the 1670s. No portrait of Lady Jane survives, so it is impossible to identify her absolutely.

The male ghost is never seen, though he is heard frequently and smelled even more often. The scent of a pungent pipe tobacco wafts through the house to proclaim his presence. There is no real evidence that this smelly pipe smoker is Sir George, but it is the identification usually given.

Smallfield

West of Lingfield is the ancient village of Smallfield, now perched beside the thundering traffic of the M23. For generations the village belonged to the Burstow family, who took their name from the hamlet a couple of miles to the south. In 1600 John Burstow built himself a beautiful stone mansion with fashionable bay windows. The house was built on the site of the old medieval moated manor which had been given to an earlier John Burstow by King Edward III as thanks for services rendered during the Hundred Years War against France. Only the western side of the moat survives, in the form of a pond, and it is here that the first ghost of Smallfield is to be found.

The phantom Lady in White has been seen standing staring into the waters of the pond with a sad and morose expression on her face. She is generally said to be dressed in her wedding dress, a fact which no doubt prompted the local story that she is some former daughter of the house who was jilted on her wedding day and then drowned herself in the pond. Unfortunately for such a tale, there are no records of a suicide in the pond and no young lady resident of the house was ever treated in such heartless fashion.

If the Lady in White is enigmatic, even more so is the Lady in Blue. This apparition is seen only in the drawing room. She is attired in a long dress of some dark blue material and strides across the room with determined step before vanishing abruptly. There is talk of a third ghost in the dining room, but some people believe her to be the Lady in Blue.

Thunderfield Castle

On the far side of the M23 from Smallfield lie the scant ruins of Thunderfield Castle, which stands beside the Haroldslea Drive off the B2036 south of Horley. It must be said that there is not all that much to see at Thunderfield Castle these days. Before the Norman Conquest, and for some years afterward, this was a quiet and unassuming manor. The name suggests that at some distant point in time it was a place sacred to the thunder god Thunor. During the anarchy that spread over England during the civil wars of King Stephen's reign, the manor was fortified by its owner, Sir Richard Clare of Tonbridge. This Sir Richard was a junior member of the powerful de Clare family, who counted four earls among its number. The Clares took the side of King Stephen against the claims of Matilda, and various members are recorded as fighting in several battles and sieges. The war did not come to Surrey in active form, so neither Thunderfield Castle nor Sir Richard were much involved.

Given the need for quick, cheap fortifications at Thunderfield, Sir Richard probably built his castle out of timber. No archaeological excavations have been carried out here, so it is impossible to be certain of how the castle originally appeared. What is clear, however, is that the timber walls and towers were strengthened by the addition of several water-filled moats. The main stronghold seems to have been an oval motte, or earthen mound, surrounded by two moats. Beside this was a larger bailey, again with a moat. Another D-shaped piece of land surrounded by a moat may have been a barbican or outwork defending the main gate, though this is unclear. What is clear is that the castle was not maintained as a serious fortification for long after the civil wars ended. The walls and towers were gradually replaced by a more peaceful manor house where the Clares could stay when visiting their estate and where the accounts and records of the lands could be kept and maintained. By about 1500 the manor was falling into disrepair, so a new house was built a short distance away at Haroldslea.

The ghosts here are an enigmatic group. The most often reported phantom manifestation is that of a bell, tolling out from the site of the castle at twilight in the autumn. Some versions have it that it tolls only on 11 November, others that it rings several times as winter draws on. On very rare occasions the bell is accompanied by a far more dramatic haunting: coming from the fields to the west of the old castle is heard the steady tramp of men on the march. The pounding footsteps get closer and closer, louder and louder until armed men come into sight through the gathering gloom. The men wear helmets and chain mail. Looking neither to left nor to right, they march steadily on towards the site of the castle. They vanish as they approach the moat.

Common sense would indicate that these ghostly soldiers should date from the civil wars that saw the castle built in the first place. Local legend, however, has it that they are almost a century older than that. Haroldslea is said to take its name from the King Harold who was killed in 1066 at the Battle of Hastings. This manor belonged to him and, it is said without any real evidence, that he stopped here for the night on his march to face the Norman invaders in Sussex. If Harold and his army did come here, they were going the long way round to get to Hastings, but that does not mean that they did not use this route south. The Weald in those days was a difficult place to cross, especially in the autumn rains. Perhaps the direct road was blocked, causing the army to take this westerly route.

Woolborough Farm

A couple of miles to the north, near Outwood, may be found Woolborough Farm, recently on the market for £1¼ million. This is a thirteenth-century farmhouse set in 7.5 acres which boasts medieval witchmarks engraved on the stone inglenook and the oak door to keep evil spirits at bay. It would seem to work as the house has not had any reports of ghosts for some years, though a century or so ago it was famous for being haunted. The house is best known for having once been the home of the poet Percy Bysshe Shelley.

Leigh Place

Further west, another ancient moated house stands overlooking the River Mole just outside the little village of Leigh. The first Leigh Place was built in the 1280s by a local landowner named John Doene, though nothing of that first house seems to remain.

The phantom reported here is that of a lady in a long gown who mooches disconsolately around the moat. A book entitled *Surrey Folklore*, published in 1893, records that she walks around the inner edge of the moat, though a more recent witness encountered her beside Leigh Place Road (which passes the moat on its western side).

One local who I quizzed about this ghost told me the following story about her. He said:

Apparently, she was a beautiful local lady from way back who was happily married to some local bigwig. They lived at Leigh Place, you see. But then her husband died in what looked like a riding accident – he was found dead in the road or some such. Anyway, a couple of years later the woman married again, this time to a chap from over Dorking direction, and she and her new husband came to live in Leigh Place. Then, some time later, the lady happened to overhear her new husband talking to one of his cronies – and she suddenly realised that the new husband had murdered her first husband. It had not been an accident at all. There was no proof, of course, so the murderer was never hanged. The poor woman pined away and died of a broken heart, and now comes back to haunt her old home.

It sounded a cracking tale, so I thought a bit of research was in order. Sadly there was no such wronged widow on record anywhere in relation to Leigh Place. But there was a not too dissimilar event. Perhaps the ghostly lady originated in the true events of 1347, and the story has altered over time as it has been passed down from generation to generation.

In 1347 the house and lands belonged to Sir Roger de Aderne, MP for Southwark and wealthy landowner. His son was a rather nasty piece of work by the name of Sir Thomas de Arderne. This Sir Thomas was a well-known local thug who robbed his neighbours, bullied them into silence and was rumoured to have murdered Nicholas de Poynings, a local landowner who had stood up to him, though nothing could be proved. In any case, his influential father refused to believe anything bad of his son and quashed any rumours.

The evil Sir Thomas went too far in 1347 when he kidnapped Lady Marjery de la Beche. This good-looking young widow held the lands of her late husband in trust for her son John until he came of age. It seems that Sir Thomas was excited as much by the lady's lands as by her good looks, but whatever his motives he dragged the young widow to the moated Leigh Place. There he tried to persuade her to marry him, using his usual brutal and violent methods. When these did not work, he raped her during the course of a drunken feast with his cronies. Lady Marjery escaped as the brutes were sleeping off the drink and fled to the local magistrate. He in turn alerted King Edward III, who sent for Sir Roger and Sir Thomas de Aderne. This time things could not be hushed up. A hefty fine was imposed on the Adernes and the king let it be known that he was watching young Sir Thomas carefully. Sir Thomas went off to fight in the wars against France, which was probably best all round, and he does not seem ever to have come back to Surrey.

The unfortunate Lady Marjery, however, did return. She was given Leigh Place and its estates by King Edward by way of compensation for her brutal treatment but she did not survive long. Whether she died of her wounds and ill treatment or of some other unconnected disease is not recorded, but pass away she did. Ever since then her ghost has been seen flitting about the grounds of Leigh Place.

The current Reigate Castle is an eighteenth-century folly built on the site of the main gateway to the public park, allegedly from the original stones. The ghost here is somewhat enigmatic and witnesses are unclear as to quite what they have seen.

Reigate

North-east of Leigh lies the lovely old town of Reigate. Unlike the moated manor houses at Leigh and elsewhere in the Weald, the castle at Reigate was a real medieval stronghold, complete with stone walls, resident nobles and battles. The structure was built on a small hill dominating both the River Mole and the Pilgrim's Way. The castle was founded by William de Warenne, a tough Norman knight who fought at the Battle of Hastings in 1066, was defeated by Hereward the Wake in 1071 and was created Earl of Surrey by William the Conqueror.

The castle had an adventurous life over the years. It last saw action in July 1648 during the English Civil War, when a force of Royalist cavalry galloped into the town and drove the Roundhead garrison back into the castle. By this date the stout walls were still standing to serve as a last refuge to the people of the town, but the internal residences and service buildings were in ruins. The Roundheads put up a stiff fight, but decided they could not withstand a long siege and fled in the night. The jubilant cavaliers marched in, led by Sir Francis Villiers. Young Villiers was brother to the Duke of Buckingham, a noted poet and reputedly the most handsome man in England. His good looks did not save him. Leading some of his men north towards Kingston upon Thames, Villiers was ambushed by Roundhead troopers and cut down. A pub called the Duke of Buckingham stands on the renamed Villiers Road to mark the spot where he died. I used to live just around the corner from the pub and knew the story of this fatal skirmish well.

Cromwell's government took steps to block any future trouble in Reigate and demolished the castle so thoroughly that no stone remained standing on top of the other – though the impressive earthwork defences remained. In 1777 a local merchant of romantic inclinations erected some mock-Gothic structures, including an impressive gateway, on the site and these are sometimes mistaken for castle ruins. Most of the old castle bailey is now a public park.

The ghost that has been reported in the castle grounds is a sadly rather insubstantial figure given the dramatic history of the fortress. I have been told of a grey figure lurking near the eighteenth-century gateway. One witness said that she thought the figure was that of a woman, but she could not be sure. Another was even vaguer, describing it as 'a grey thing that glided away through the arch. I only saw it for a moment.'

Rather more definite was the phantom that plagued Knight's in Bell Street. More properly known as James Knight's Department Store, Knight's has been a much-loved fixture of the Reigate shopping scene for generations. The store recently had a makeover to take it successfully into the twenty-first century. It does not seem to have done much to shift the ghost, however.

The older part of the store was formerly a coaching inn before it was converted and the store has since spread out to include several neighbouring buildings that were variously houses, shops and workshops. Rumour has it that this was one of the less respectable hotels in Reigate and that it became notorious in the early nineteenth century for its loose morals and prostitutes. Be that as it may, the staff at Knight's have reported a variety of odd experiences over the years. The most persistent report is that of a small boy aged around eight years old. He is said to have died in the building when it was a hotel and there are persistent rumours of foul play. Whether he was mistreated and succumbed to disease or deliberately murdered is not entirely clear, but he is generally held to have been an unwanted child of a Reigate prostitute who scraped by, running errands for those who ran the hotel. More enigmatic is the lady in a purple dress who has been reported. Nobody seems to know anything at all about her.

Tucked behind Bell Street is Reigate Priory – like the castle this is also now a public park. Bell Street takes its name from the curfew bell rung in the Priory Gatehouse during medieval times. The priory was built in about 1245 by the Crutched Friars, an enigmatic order of holy men who wore a blue habit, on the chest of which was stitched a red cross. The order originated in what is now Syria in about AD 250, opened an office in Rome in 1169 and gradually spread across Europe. They were never either wealthy or numerous and in 1656 Pope Alexander VII forced them to merge with the Augustinians. By that date, of course, the Reigate Priory had been closed down by King Henry VIII as part of the sixteenth-century Reformation. The Priory and its estates were sold to the Howard family, famously resident in Effingham, who converted the buildings into a house. They sold the place in 1681 and the house subsequently passed through various hands and saw much demolition and building work before it was bought by the town council. The house to be seen today is eighteenth century in date and the foundations of the medieval priory lie beneath the lawns to the south.

The ghost that has been reported here is that of a priest – though romantics would have it that he is really a medieval friar. The park was totally and impressively refurbished in 2008, with a large children's playground being installed. I take my daughter there often, but have never found anyone who has seen anything even remotely spectral. Nevertheless, rumours persist and nearly everyone is convinced that the grounds of the old Priory really are haunted.

A couple of hundred yards east of the Priory stands St Mary's Church in Chart Lane. There has been a church here since at least 1160, and possibly for some three centuries longer. The oldest part of the structure standing today is the nave, which dates to around 1270, with the chancel being added a century later and vestry and library being added in the eighteenth century. Disaster almost struck in 1820 when a new and enthusiastic vicar had the buttresses and internal ties removed to open up the interior of the church. As a result the walls began to bend and the roof sagged alarmingly. Only drastic remedial work in 1828 saved the day.

The first of the ghosts here would seem to date to about the time of the nineteenth-century work. She is a young lady dressed in a loose, flowing gown who walks with sprightly step from the church towards the lych gate. She is mostly seen on the path inside the churchyard, but a few people claim to have seen her emerging from the lych gate onto Chart Lane, where she vanishes.

Encountered rather more often are the phantom singers of St Mary. The best-known appearance of the singers came in 1975 when local lady Mrs Christine Bell was walking past in the early evening. She was puzzled to hear the sounds of the congregation singing from inside the church, for the building was dark and unlit. Mrs Bell was happy to retell her experiences to the press, and though others have also heard the singing they have been less inclined to speak in public. One young lady, who preferred not to be named, told me about her experience, which took place late one summer's evening in 2003:

I had been in town with some friends drinking and we were walking home. We stopped here and sat down on that bench for a chat and a rest. We'd been here a few minutes, I suppose, when we heard the sound of singing coming from inside the church. It was really spooky as the church was dark and there were no lights or anything. One of the lads decided somebody was playing a trick on us. He got up and went to the church door to bang on it and shout out to see who was there. But we were too scared to let him do it. We dragged him away from the door and that was when the singing stopped. We hung about for a bit to see if anyone came out the church or if anyone was going to leap out and say, 'Ha ha, we tricked you'. But there was nobody. It was just eerie and quiet. So we left. It wasn't until a couple of days later, when I told my dad what had happened, that I heard the church was supposed to be haunted. At the time we didn't think it was ghosts, we just thought it was a bit odd.

I have also heard tales of a ghostly soldier patrolling the ramparts of what is generally known as Reigate Fort. This squat defensive work was built in 1898 as tension with Germany began to mount. It was designed as a defensive redoubt to guard the main road running north to London (now the A217) as it climbs up out of Reigate to scale the steep face of the North Downs. The buildings were also used as a vast magazine store in which guns and ammunition were kept for the use of the local yeomanry regiment and to resupply any troops posted along the North Downs in the event of an invasion. The fort now belongs to the National Trust and is open, free of charge, year round, though guided tours take place at times in the summer. It lies squeezed between the A217 and the M25 and is approached by a footpath from the small car park and café at the top end of Wray Lane, beside Gatton Park.

The phantom sentry is usually described as being a somewhat shadowy figure in a tall hat and I have been unable to find anyone who has got a good view of him.

The Wray Lane that runs down the hill from the car park near the fort to Reigate passes through wooded lands until it emerges near the foot of the hill to cross open land and then plunge into a housing estate on the north-eastern edge of Reigate. This route is said to be haunted by two ghosts. The first is an elderly man wearing large boots that make a distinctive clumping noise as he walks. Some say the boots are old-fashioned high riding boots. The other ghost is that of a young girl, aged perhaps ten or so, who has long blonde hair dressed in ringlets. Whether the two are connected or not is unknown. They do not seem ever to have appeared together, at any rate.

Reigate Heath

South-west of Reigate, the Flanchford Road peels off the A25 Buckland Road to cross Reigate Heath. This stretch of open country is now home to a golf course and is a considerably tamer place than it was in days gone by. I have picked up only one report of the ghost here, and she does not seem to be very well known. The witness I met told me the following:

> I was out walking when I saw this woman coming toward me. I thought there was something odd about her, but she did not float about in mid-air or anything like ghosts are meant to do. I glanced at her again and she just vanished. One second she was there, the next she was gone.

The sighting took place on the path that runs from Flanchford Road to the golf clubhouse.

I would not usually include a one-off sighting of this kind. It is all too easy for a person to make a simple mistake. They may see a perfectly normal human being walking over a common, take their eyes off them momentarily and find that they have 'vanished' when in fact they have simply stepped into a hollow in the ground that cannot be easily seen. Other mistakes are also easily made. One famous example from the 1930s involved a 'lady in white' who was seen by several witnesses in a field in Hertfordshire at twilight. Each witness reported the same thing: a figure in white that came rushing towards them from the edge of the field as they climbed over the stile that carried a footpath into the field. An intrepid reporter from the local newspaper was sent to investigate. Instead of running away as the others had done, he stood his ground and discovered the 'lady in white' to be a particularly large and aggressive goose.

However, this particular witness is known to me and is adamant that she saw the figure of the phantom lady disappear right in front of her eyes. 'I was looking right at her when she vanished. It was like a light being switched off. Click, she was gone.' So with the usual caveats about single witness reports, I include the ghost here.

Buckland

Just west of Reigate Heath, along the A25, stands the village of Buckland. West of the village the road crosses the small Shag Brook, a tributary of the River Mole. The word 'shag' is derived from an old Saxon word that translates as 'demon', 'monster' or 'evil', depending on its context. It is no great surprise, therefore, to learn that the Shag Brook had an unpleasant reputation in days gone by. There were numerous reports of horses that refused to cross the ford that existed here until Victorian times. Others reported that cattle would not drink from the stream. But the most often related tale said that a hideous monster lurked at the ford across the Shag Brook.

In most versions of the story the beast lived under or beside a standing stone that once stood some 10ft tall beside the ford. The creature was said to take the form of a hairy ape-like man of great size and enormous strength. It had 6in talons on its hands and even longer razor-sharp teeth that it bared when enraged. One man who dared to brave the monster was a Reigate man who joined the cavalry to fight Napoleon and returned home after the Battle of Waterloo full of bravado and tales of the wars. Perhaps inevitably he was challenged to cross the ford after dark, and with some trepidation set out on his charger to do so. It was not long before he was back, shaking with fear. He claimed to have completed the feat, but that the monster had appeared and came splashing towards him, upon which he fled.

In the later nineteenth century, the road was widened and the standing stone taken away – it is now missing, which is no doubt a great loss to archaeology. Some say that the local workmen refused to start work on a bridge over the brook until the ford had been blessed by the vicar of Reigate. Either way, the beast has not been seen since the work was done.

There are those who would treat this tale not as a ghost story but as an example of folklore. Given that the stream has a name derived from a word for a demon, it is not unlikely that the waterway was one of those that in pagan times was held to be sacred to some old English god. The early Christian missionaries frequently denounced the old gods as being demons and chastised those who still honoured them as demon-worshippers. It was all part of the propaganda drive to persuade the English to follow the worship of Christ. Perhaps the standing stone, the ford and the sacred stream made up some pagan worshipping place of great power. Perhaps that power was remembered by subsequent generations as a demonic monster of awesome power. Perhaps.

Ockley

Some miles to the south-west, the village of Ockley stands astride the old Roman road from London to Chichester, later called Stane Street and now the A29, as it leaves the Downs behind to the north and strikes off across the Weald. Overlooking the village green is the aptly named Inn on the Green, formerly the Red Lion. This fine old fifteenth-century inn was once a coaching inn, but now offers accommodation; it is one of Surrey's leading gastro-pubs. It even has that most modern of conveniences: free wi-fi throughout.

The phantom, however, is rather older than the modern facilities that the inn now boasts. Back in the later Victorian period, a young lady was thrown from her horse when she was fox hunting nearby. Her injuries did not seem to be particularly serious, so her friends accompanied her to the inn so she could rest until she felt well enough to ride home. Unexpectedly, the lady passed away. Only then was it realised that she had suffered internal injuries that, although not especially painful, had proved fatal. The ghost of the unfortunate lady has been seen walking about the pub ever since.

One witness who saw her in 2009 told me that she was rather short, with dark hair and a long dress that had a tight body but voluminous skirts. He saw the ghost from behind, so he could not describe her face, but he did somehow get the impression that she was a gentle soul. The landlord's dog acted rather oddly on several occasions in 2010, watching intently and sometimes barking at some moving object that no human could see.

Although the fatal riding accident is usually blamed for the haunting, another puzzle appeared when renovation work was taking place in 1999. The bar ceiling had been bowing down for some years and the then landlord decided to take the opportunity of having it pulled down and replaced entirely. When the workmen were taking down the plaster and lathes, they found a cache of bones stashed away at one end of the room. These turned out to be human, but there was not a complete skeleton present. The bones were given a decent burial. Whether or not the bones had any bearing on the haunting was never very clear. Certainly their discovery and removal had no effect on the ghost, so it seems that they were probably unconnected.

One of the houses on the other side of the A29 from the inn is said to be haunted by a young lady accompanied by a little girl. The two are remarkably active and are seen frequently by the owner of the house.

Peaslake

North-west of Ockley is Peaslake, where a helpful ghost by the name of Johnny Upfold used to be active. This character was a friendly soul who helped out with household tasks, but only if nobody was watching him. If spoken to he fled. He would thus seem to be a local manifestation of the more helpful members of the fairy race, sometimes called brownies. These little people helped with household tasks so long as they were well treated, but if annoyed were able to sour milk, spoil butter and generally make life difficult for rural households. However, before Johnny Upfold is dismissed as a piece of fairylore, it is worth remarking that the Upfolds were, and are, a very real local family. There is even an Upfold Farm just four miles to the east. Perhaps there once was a Johnny Upfold who has come to be remembered as a helpful little sprite around Peaslake.

Cranleigh

To the south of Peaslake lies the town of Cranleigh, and just outside to the south-east stands Baynards Park. This is the haunt of the ghost of one of the most famous men said to return to Surrey in spectral form: Sir Thomas More. More was born in 1478 into the family of a well-to-do lawyer in London. As a boy he showed himself to be quite remarkably intelligent, hard working and religiously devout. He considered

Sir Thomas More came from a relatively obscure family, but by hard work and application worked his way up to the pinnacle of Tudor society before falling foul of Henry VIII and ending up on the scaffold. His head was later taken to Cranleigh and his ghost haunts Baynards Park.

becoming a priest, but instead went into his father's legal profession and married in 1505, and again in 1511, having five daughters in all.

He undertook some legal work for the government and so came to the notice of the young King Henry VIII, who gave him a series of jobs and positions. More was also a prolific writer, producing a number of histories and religious or philosophical works of which *Utopia* – describing an idealised society – is the best known. In 1529, Henry made More Lord Chancellor, a position that put him at the head of the government bureaucracy and gave him wide-ranging powers and great wealth. However, More opposed the move by Henry that made the King of England the head of the Church of England, believing instead that the Pope should be the head of a united Church covering all of Christendom. In 1532 More resigned as Lord Chancellor rather than take an oath required of all government servants that recognised the king as head of the Church.

More then made the error of not clearly condemning the prophecies issued by a nun from Kent named Elizabeth Barton, better known to history as the Holy Maid of Kent. Barton claimed her messages came from the Virgin Mary, and, although her early prophecies concerned only local people and events, she went on to condemn the break with Rome and prophesy the imminent death of King Henry. She was quickly arrested and hanged for treason. Henry regarded More's refusal to condemn the prophecies as indicating that he believed them to be true. More was also arrested. The trial that followed was one of the first judicial murders perpetrated by Henry. The charges of treason were clearly false, but Henry could not execute More for his real crime of not recognising the king's new marriage to Anne Boleyn. The jury was composed of relatives of Anne Boleyn and servants of the king, so there was never any doubt of the verdict. More was executed on Tower Hill on 6 July 1535. His body was buried in the Church of St Peter ad Vincula; his head was put on a spike over the gate of the Tower of London, where it served as a warning to all those who dared defy the king.

So far More had no real connection with Surrey, other than to travel through it from time to time. But his daughter Margaret had married William Roper, a wealthy Surrey landowner who lived at Baynards

Park. Sometime in August, More's head went missing from the spike at the Tower. A half-hearted search was conducted, but the missing head was never found. It had, in fact, been obtained by young Margaret, who had bribed a guard at the Tower. The head was hidden in a sealed panel somewhere at Baynards for the next nine years. When Margaret died in 1544 she was buried in the Roper family vault at St Dunstan's Church in Canterbury. Her father's head was buried with her, cradled in her arms.

It seems to have been those years when the severed head of More was kept at Baynards that prompted the haunting. The figure of Sir Thomas has been seen for generations walking about the grounds of the house. Those who have seen him say that he seemed to be searching for something – presumably his head.

Dunsfold Aerodrome

On the other side of Cranleigh lies Dunsfold Aerodrome. This airfield was built in 1942 by the Canadian Air Force and served as a base for B25 Mitchell bombers until 1946, when it was sold by the government to the Hawker Aircraft Co., which used it to test the revolutionary Hunter jet fighter. The airfield was sold again in 2002 to a private company which uses the place for a variety of purposes. The Surrey Air Ambulance service is based at Dunsfold, film companies use it as a set for scenes taking place at airports and, probably most famously, the BBC TV programme *Top Gear* is made here.

The haunting of the site centres on a decommissioned Boeing 747 jumbo jet which is parked at Dunsfold and is used in

The ghost of Dunsfold Aerodrome appears in the rather incongruous surroundings of a decommissioned British Airways Boeing 747 jumbo jet.

The jolly monk of the Grantley Arms at Wonersh is one of the most popular ghosts in Surrey as he seems to exude good humour and a hearty welcome to visitors.

film and television work. It cannot fly, but does taxi about the runways during filming. Designated GBDXJ, the aircraft formerly flew with British Airways from 1980 to 2002. On one of its later flights, the aircraft had the misfortune to carry a lady passenger who suffered a heart attack on board. She was declared dead on arrival at hospital. It is this lady who haunts the aircraft and its immediate surroundings. She was particularly active when the aircraft was used during the filming of the 007 film *Casino Royale*. She was reported walking along the aisles of the jet and sitting in a seat.

Wonersh

Altogether more amiable than most ghosts in Surrey is the ghost to be found at the Grantley Arms in Wonersh. He goes by the name of the Jolly Monk, and his appearance and behaviour more than live up to this name. The pub in part occupies a building put up about 1410 to serve as a hostelry for visitors to a nearby monastery. When the Reformation came, King Henry VIII sold off the monastic properties and the building became a private house. In the 1760s it was inhabited by Sir Fletcher Norton, who was not only MP for Surrey but went on to become the Speaker of the House of Commons. When he stood down from Parliament he was created Baron Grantley – a title still held by his descendants as well as by the pub that now occupies his old home.

The Jolly Monk dates back to the days when this was a monastic hostelry. He is described as being dressed pretty much as you would expect of a monk, in long brown habit and hood. He seems to be happy enough and exudes a welcoming atmosphere. For some years, however, the Jolly Monk was less than happy around Christmas time. He was held to be responsible for pulling down the pub's Christmas decorations, overturning Christmas trees and generally making a nuisance of himself. An Irish barmaid who was living upstairs decided to take a hand. She held a ceremony of some kind that she claimed was a traditional Irish exorcism. The Jolly Monk promptly stopped tearing down the tinsel, but he has also stopped turning up at all. I am told he has not been seen for some twenty-five years now.

A few steps west of the pub stands the ancient Church of St John the Baptist, the oldest parts of which date to around 1050. I have heard different accounts of the

The path leading to the church at Wonersh is widely reported to be haunted, but the different accounts vary so widely that it is difficult to be certain what is being reported.

Back in 1901, a man named George Smithers died at the Percy Arms in Childworth. Fifty years later, the pub was struck by an outbreak of poltergeist activity – but was the unfortunate Mr Smithers to blame?

haunting here and there is little consistency between them. The only thing on which all accounts seem to agree is that something rather unpleasant is sometimes encountered on the path leading from The Street to the churchyard proper. What it is is disputed, but it is not very nice.

Chilworth

North of Wonersh stands the village of Chilworth with, at its heart, the Percy Arms pub, now famous for its food. In 1951 the pub was the scene of a short-lived but quite spectacular outburst of poltergeist activity. It began just as head waiter Bernard Wilson was going to bed upstairs after closing up for the night. There suddenly came the sound of the bar shutters being violently shaken back and forth. Thinking burglars were trying to get at the till, Wilson grabbed a fire poker and raced downstairs to confront them. The noise ceased as he pounded down the stairs and when he reached the bar, all was quiet and still. Thereafter the disturbances began in earnest.

When Wilson came down in the morning objects in the bar were often found in strange places: glasses on the floor and chairs on tables. Then the objects began to move when the pub was open. On one famous occasion a bar stool lifted itself up into the air and floated some 5ft towards the door before gently coming to rest, and all in front of the amazed gaze of more than a dozen customers. After some weeks of flying glasses, shaking tables and moving chairs the trouble ceased.

At the time, the disturbances were blamed on the ghost of an unfortunate man named George Smithers, who had died in the pub in 1901 after an accident at a nearby factory. The doctor had been unable to do anything for him, so serious were his injuries. However, it is unlikely that the phantom of Smithers was involved, as poltergeists seem to be a quite different type of entity from a ghost.

Bramley

To the west lies the large village of Bramley. A shop in the High Street is supposed to be haunted by the ghost of a young girl, but I have been unable to find anyone who claims to have seen her in the past forty years, and in any case the current owners of the shop did not seem too keen on ghostly stories. More certain is the haunting of the woods up on Chinthurst Hill, a notable landmark just north of the village. An elderly woman dressed in a shawl leads a horse out of the woods on to Chinthurst Lane and turns north before vanishing. Some say she is a gypsy, but there does not seem to be much evidence for this other than her shawl and horse.

A tsar of Russia, no less, is blamed for the haunting of the Kings Arms and Royal in Godalming. It is certain that Tsar Peter the Great once stayed here, but altogether less certain that he is the cause of the supernatural trouble.

Godalming

West again is the town of Godalming. The Kings Arms & Royal Hotel stands in the High Street, dominating it almost. The oldest parts of the building go back to 1358 and it is rumoured that Henry VIII once stayed here. More reliable is the fact that Admiral Nelson slept here several times on his way from London to Portsmouth and back again. Another guest, and one that left his spectral mark, was Tsar Peter the Great of Russia, who came here in 1698. In theory, the tsar was travelling incognito, but everyone knew who he was. The good folk of Godalming were appalled by his drunken carousing, rude behaviour and dirty clothing. After a riotous and rather destructive stay at the hotel, the tsar and his entourage paid their bills and moved on.

The visit obviously made a major impact, for Peter has been blamed for the haunting of the hotel. The ghost is never seen, which might make the identification a bit suspect, but is heard often. The sound of a man wearing heavy boots enters the room where Peter slept on his visit. The boots are heard to walk across the room and the man to sit down. The boots are removed and fall with heavy thuds on to the floor. Then silence reigns.

Another royal visitor has been blamed for the supernatural events at Godalming's Westbrook Place, this time the royal in question being Bonnie Prince Charlie, but once again his guilt for the events is far from certain.

The wide meadows on the north side of the Rive Wey at Godalming are known as the Lammas Lands. Here too there is a ghost that is heard, not seen. On the morning of 11 November 1817, Godalming merchant and carter George Chennell failed to turn up for work. One of his employees went to the old man's house in the High Street to see if he was ill or needed assistance. He found the front door bolted and got no reply. The back door, however, was open. In the kitchen the luckless employee found the body of Chennell's housekeeper, Elizabeth Wilson. Her throat had been cut. When the magistrates arrived, they ventured upstairs and found the dead body of Chennell himself, also with a cut throat. The house had been ransacked and stripped of silver, cash and other objects of value.

Soon afterwards a local woman of known criminal habits came to the magistrates and told them she wanted to turn king's evidence. She said that she had been hired to act as look out for a burglary, but had not realised until the following day that the burglars had murdered the house's inhabitants. She named the burglars as a known local thief William Chalcraft and Chennell's own son, George Chennell junior. The two men were hanged in the Lammas Lands after a short trial.

The ghostly sounds are those of a cart lumbering over the turf, a cheering crowd and the ominous creaking of rope on wood.

Westbrook Place

Just outside the town stands Westbrook Place, a grand manor now a corporate headquarters. The grounds are said to be haunted by an enigmatic man in a cloak who appears only on moonlit nights. This figure is generally said to be the phantom of Charles Edward Stuart, better known to history as Bonnie Prince Charlie. After the bloody failure of his rebellion in 1745 the young prince fled to France, but came to Britain using a false identity some years later. Westbrook is one of the houses that he visited.

Wormley

At Wormley, south of Godalming, stands the King Edward VI School. The buildings are said to be haunted by the ghost of a former pupil who died on the premises. Details seem rather vague about this death. According to one version the hapless boy died of some disease that has now been largely tamed by science – scarlet fever or some such – though a second version has it that he died when he fell from a great height to which he had climbed for a dare. However the child died, he returns to haunt the main staircase, appearing as a pale, drawn child of about fourteen years of age.

Waverley Abbey

A few miles east, just off the B3001 as it crosses the River Wey, stand the ruins of Waverley Abbey. It might be expected that the ruins would play host to the ghost of a monk or two, and this is indeed the case. This particular monk is said to have been killed by ruthless men seeking to make him give the location of a buried treasure. The ghostly monk comes back, it is said, to make sure that his precious hoard remains intact. According to one witness, the monk wore a red habit. This would make him a cardinal, a high-ranking cleric indeed.

The most likely date for such an event would be the dissolution of the abbey by

The red monk of Waverley is one of the most persistent of
Surrey's ghosts, but who he was and why he haunts the ruins
are matters of great dispute.

Henry VIII in 1536. Elsewhere monks did indeed seek to hide holy relics, precious ritual ware and other objects from the king's commissioners, though it must be said that this was a rare event and so far as is known not a single monk was killed during the Dissolution itself – though quite a few were to fall foul of Henry's religious laws later on. The records show that the thirteen monks of Waverley handed over their abbey and its estates in return for pensions without any protest. Perhaps the bloody events behind the haunting date to some other period.

Ash

The rectory at Ash, just to the north, was built on what had formerly been the main road, the route of which was altered when the Basingstoke Canal was built in 1794. It is this that is generally taken to be the explanation for the extraordinary haunting of Ash Rectory. After a disturbed night in 1938, the rector wrote:

> I was woken by the thud of horses' hooves and the sound of a horn. The coach came in the back way and drove straight through the house and made towards the church. I saw the coachman distinctly. He was wearing a scarlet seventeenth or eighteenth-century uniform. He seemed quite a cheerful person, and I am distinctly under the impression that he turned around as I gazed after him and gave me a cheery wave with his whip. I have not seen this phantom coach since, but I do not mind if I do. If the Rectory must have a ghost, it is as well that it should be a jolly one.

I was told that this spectacular ghost can be seen only once, for the same person never sees it twice, which seems something of a shame.

Not far away stands Ash Manor, a pleasant house dating back in parts to the fourteenth century. In 1934 a Mr and Mrs Kelly moved in with their teenage daughter Patricia. Within days the Kellys began to hear footsteps, moans and muttering voices. The sounds seem to come most often from the main staircase and from the main bedroom on the first floor, but whenever Mr Kelly went to investigate there was nobody to be seen. Finally, Mr Kelly managed to corner the intruder. Racing to the bedroom on hearing footsteps, Mr Kelly saw a short man in a shabby green coat near the window. Mr Kelly lunged forward, only for the man to vanish into thin air in front of his eyes. It was then that the Kellys had to accept that they had a haunting on their hands.

Mr Kelly sent for a noted psychic named Mrs Eileen Garrett, who held a séance in the bedroom. Garrett made contact with the spirit of a man who had been captured during a skirmish in the Wars of the Roses in the later fifteenth century. He had been dragged to Ash Manor, where he was clapped into irons and held prisoner. The unfortunate man died in chains and had been lurking around the house looking for revenge. Garrett said that she persuaded him to leave the manor and seek out his family. The haunting did peter out after the séance.

Farnham

A couple of miles south-west of Ash lies Farnham, arguably the most densely haunted patch of Surrey. It is just a shame that so little is known about most of the spectral visitors.

Any tour of haunted Farnham has to start at the castle, which was first built in 1138 by Henry, Bishop of Winchester. It was changed and adapted many times over the years as it served as the main stronghold of the bishops of Winchester. After being held for King Charles I during the Civil Wars of the 1640s, the castle was slighted - meaning that its defences were rendered useless by being blown apart by gunpowder. Unlike most other slighted castles, Farnham was not abandoned completely.

In 1662, George Morley became Bishop of Winchester and set about restoring the shattered castle to be a comfortable mansion and administrative centre combined. It is appropriate, therefore, that it is Morley's ghost which haunts the Fox Tower. He is also given the credit for the spectral bells that sometimes ring out from the old keep. A second ghost is to be found in the Great Hall. It is of a man in a long cloak, usually identified as a monk, though he could as easily be a cleric of almost any kind. The stairs leading to the hall are haunted by a young girl who dances or skips about when she appears. The gateway to the castle is haunted by two quite different ghosts. The first is a young lady in a fawn-coloured gown that reaches down to the floor. She seems harmless enough, but not so the bizarre shapeless apparition that seems to climb up walls and inspires stark terror in those unfortunate enough to meet it.

Castle Street runs from the castle down to the town and is said to be haunted by a coach pulled by four horses. It trots up the hill, then comes to a halt by the roadside. The door opens and down steps a gentleman dressed in the fashions of the very early nineteenth century. This gent is usually said to be the worse for drink, for he staggers about as if inebriated before he and the coach vanish. The Castle Theatre once stood in Castle Street. This was haunted by the ghost of a tall man, variously described as a suicide or a murderer, who was blamed for the persistent electrical problems in the building.

West Street, Farnham, is haunted by a spectral pet dog that scampers about, apparently perfectly content with its lot.

Farnham Library is housed in an ancient house which once played host to a most distinguished royal visitor, who was also a prisoner. His ghost is said to remain here centuries after he himself left.

At the foot of the hill, West Street runs off to the right. This pleasant road is haunted by a black dog. This is not the spectral hound that terrifies people in other parts of England, but a pet dog. Some think it is owned by the ghostly old woman who is also to be seen in West Street. The two may or may not be connected. The ghostly woman is seen only when it is raining, while the dog may appear at any time.

Further along West Street stands Vernon House, now the Farnham Library and Museum. Back in January 1649 it was a comfortable private house, the largest residence in the town since the castle was at that time mostly in ruins and not yet rebuilt. So when King Charles I came to Farnham, it was natural that he should stay here. Not that he had much choice in the matter, since he was under heavy armed guard while being moved from comfortable house arrest at Windsor Castle to his trial and execution in London. Charles was not kept in Vernon House for long, but it seems that it was for long enough to leave a spectral mark. The figure of a short, slight man with dark hair who has been seen here is usually identified by witnesses as being the phantom of the luckless king.

The Lion and Lamb Hotel used to stand in West Street, but has now been replaced by a little mews of shops. The hotel was haunted by a very active ghost, that of a lady who was seen walking about the restaurant area up to two or three times a day. She has not been seen since the hotel closed. Also gone is the old Hop Bag, formerly a coaching inn and more recently a pub. The ghost here, however, remains. A horse clatters into the yard, then vanishes.

South of the eastern end of West Street stands St Andrew's Church. There have been several odd manifestations here. The sounds of a male choir singing hymns when the church is empty have been reported several times, as have the sounds of a vicar and congregation praying. An elderly lady is often seen walking up the path to the church, only to vanish at the threshold of the church. Those who have seen her report that her lips are moving as if she is chatting away quite happily to a friend, but no words can be heard. Rather more unusual was the semi-transparent veil or screen that a visitor saw descend from the roof to cut off the chancel from the nave. Behind the veil, the chancel seemed to be thronged with equally transparent people. Both the veil and the figures vanished abruptly.

If instead of turning right at the foot of the hill into West Street, you were to turn left, you would enter The Borough, the town's busiest shopping street. Here stands the Bush Hotel, now part of the Mercure chain. This has been a hotel, guest house or pub for some 750 years, and it is impossible to be certain to which date the ghost belongs. She is an elderly woman who is seen on the first floor pottering in and out of the rooms as if making sure that everything is in order.

Bourne Mill, now a shop, on the Guildford Road is said to be haunted by a remarkably pretty young woman dressed in the heavy silks of the eighteenth century.

Tilford

South-east of Farnham stands the little village of Tilford, best known for its twin medieval bridges over the Wey that replaced the eponymous ford. The ghost here is an odd one, for it is that of a donkey! The unfortunate beast was one of several kept by a man who lived on Charles Hill. He earned a living by renting his donkeys, horses and oxen out to passing carters and coachmen to help them haul their vehicles up the steep hill. One day a donkey was given too hard a task and collapsed and died – and before long its ghost began to be seen plodding morosely up the hill. An enterprising local promptly renamed his nearby pub, the Halfway House, The Donkey. The pub is still there, serving tasty meals to anyone who calls. The current owners have bought a pair of donkeys which are proving to be great favourites with children.

South-east of Tilford, the pleasant village of Chiddingfold stands astride the A283. The green is dominated by the ancient Crown Inn. Parts of this building are 700 years old, for it was built as a guest house by the Cistercian order of monks for those on pilgrimage or on Cistercian business. There are rumours of a ghostly monk in the inn, but he does not seem to have been seen recently. Also gone is the poltergeist who caused quite a bit of the usual nuisance expected of such things back in the 1960s.

Lythe Hill

To the south-west, the village of Lythe Hill stands on the B2131 as that road drops down towards Haslemere to the west. The luxurious Lythe Hill Hotel offers spa facilities and sumptuous dining. It also offers customers a 'spook-buster' upgrade. Anyone who sleeps in the haunted bedroom, named the Katherine of Aragon Suite, can borrow an infra-red camera, a motion detector, a digital thermometer and other technical gear often used by ghosthunters to try to record the presence of something unusual.

There can be few more pleasant ways to investigate the paranormal than to snuggle down into the lap of luxury with all the latest high-tech ghost detecting gear.

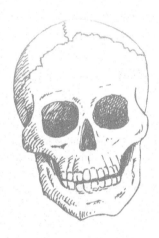

Other titles published by The History Press

Paranormal Surrey
RUPERT MATTHEWS

The county of Surrey may wear a face of suburban and rural normality, but lurking not far below the surface is an unequalled amount of paranormal activity and strangeness. In this volume, local author Rupert Matthews, an expert on the subject of the paranormal, draws together a terrifying and intriguing collection of first-hand accounts and long-forgotten archive reports from the county's history.

978 0 7524 5422 1

The Little Book of the Paranormal
RUPERT MATTHEWS

This little book introduces the reader to the world of the paranormal and entertains them with numerous anecdotes, snippets of information and lists of events. Including chapters on UFOs and aliens, Bigfoot and man-apes, ghosts and hauntings, sea-serpents and lake monsters, predictions and curses, poltergeists, paranormal humans as well as near-death experiences and mediumship, this is a thought-provoking book covering all aspects of the paranormal in an accessible and entertaining way.

978 0 7524 5165 7

Haunted Hampshire
RUPERT MATTHEWS

This well-researched tour around Hampshire showcases almost 100 ghostly encounters. Here you will discover ghostly seamen haunting the King's Bastion at Portsmouth, spirits of the Roundheads galloping through Crondall and a haunted megalith at Mottistone. Each entry includes not just the story of the ghost but also eerie eyewitness accounts. Exploring everything from pubs and churchyards to castles and ports, *Haunted Hampshire* will appeal to anyone interested in the supernatural history of the area.

978 0 7524 4862 6

The Little Book of Surrey
RUPERT MATTHEWS

The Little Book of Surrey is a funny, fast-paced, fact-packed compendium of the sort of frivolous, fantastic or simply strange information which no one will want to be without. The county's most unusual crimes and punishments, eccentric inhabitants, famous sons and daughters, royal connections and literally hundreds of wacky facts about Surrey's landscape, towns and villages (plus some authentically bizarre bits of historic trivia), come together to make it essential reading for visitors and locals alike.

978 0 7524 5633 1

Visit our website and discover thousands of other History Press books.
www.thehistorypress.co.uk